THIRD EDITION

Skills for Success
READING AND WRITING

Jennifer Bixby

Teacher's Handbook
WITH TEACHER ACCESS CARD

OXFORD
UNIVERSITY PRESS

Great Clarendon Street, Oxford, OX2 6DP, United Kingdom

Oxford University Press is a department of the University of Oxford.
It furthers the University's objective of excellence in research, scholarship,
and education by publishing worldwide. Oxford is a registered trade
mark of Oxford University Press in the UK and in certain other countries

ISBN: 978 0 19 499906 9   Pack
ISBN: 978 0 19 499907 6   Teacher's Handbook

Printed in China

This book is printed on paper from certified and well-managed sources

ACKNOWLEDGEMENTS

Back cover photograph: Oxford University Press building/David Fisher

CONTENTS

Teaching with Q: Skills for Success Third Edition

Professional development articles to help you teach with
Q: Skills for Success Third Edition.

Critical Thinking Foundations: Implications for the Language Classroom

James D. Dunn Q Series Consultant, Critical Thinking Skills
Junior Associate Professor - Tokai University
Coordinator - Japan Association for Language Teaching, Critical Thinking
Special Interest Group

Critical Thinking has become a buzzword in education over the past decade (Finnish National Board of Education, 2004; Moore, 2013; Mulnix, 2012; Scriven & Paul, 2007) and for good reason—it is a very important skill for life. But how should we, as educators, best integrate critical thinking into our language learning classroom? This article will give a working definition of critical thinking, shed light on the foundations of critical thinking, and provide some concrete avenues to introduce it into your classroom.

What is Critical Thinking?

It can be very difficult to get a good grasp on what critical thinking is because it can be a particularly nebulous concept, made up of sub-objects which form the foundation of what most people envision as critical thinking (Scriven & Paul, 2007; van Gelder, 2005). To understand critical thinking, we need to first understand what it is made up of. The building blocks of critical thinking are higher-order thinking skills (HOTS). These skills, which are the fundamental skills utilized during the process of critical thinking (Dalton, 2011; Ford & Yore, 2012), are essential to understand in order to start students on the path toward being critical thinkers. Textbooks like *Q: Skills for Success Third Edition*, which integrate language practice that focuses on the implementation and development of HOTS in a second language, help to enable students to become more critical thinkers.

What are Higher-Order Thinking Skills?

Higher-order thinking skills are derived from Bloom's Revised Taxonomy (Krathwohl, 2002) which gives us a simplified, yet powerful, way to look at how students use their brains to remember, process, and use information (Fig. 1). The top three sections of Bloom's Revised Taxonomy are what many consider the higher-order thinking skills, or activities, if you will. One of the best uses for the taxonomy is attributing verbs to each tier in order to help an educator build activities that utilize these skills. Each skill has a myriad of verbs that comprise the level of thinking which, when integrated into a textbook, help students develop their understanding of a new language, and also foster the ability to think more critically about the information presented to them in the classroom or even in life.

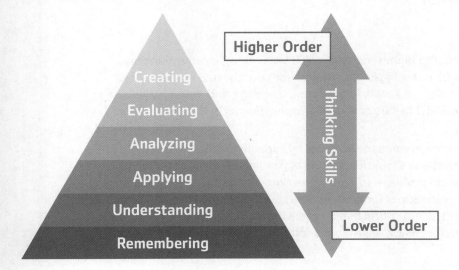

Fig. 1: Bloom's Revised Taxonomy

CRITICAL THINKING

The verbs that are associated with the higher-order thinking skills are essential for developing the potential for critical thinking. The following are a few verbs, with activity suggestions that come from *Q: Skills for Success*, for the higher-order thinking skills that you can use in your classroom.

Analyzing

Analysis in language learning has a few beneficial effects. First, students are introduced to using their own judgement in the process of learning a new language. This helps in the development of pattern recognition and familiarization with the structure of knowledge. This aids in the student's ability to distinguish between items, recognize fact or opinion, and compare and contrast items. These skills are valuable in the production of both written and spoken English.

One way to integrate analyzing into language learning is to have students order information by a metric. Students are given a list of data and are asked to organize it into an order. This order could be derived from categories, a hierarchy, a taxonomy (like Bloom's), time, location, and importance. This can be further developed into a more challenging task by asking students to distinguish data from a series of similar information. With words that are similar in meaning to each other being used in the same text, it could be beneficial for students to practice differentiating these words and identifying how they differ from each other. Words like *tasty* and *mouth-watering* are very similar but have different depth or connotations.

You can push these activities to have a critical-thinking bent to them by asking the students to justify and explain their organization of data to a partner or a group. By explaining their thought process on how they organized the information, they open themselves up to questions and deeper reflection on how they used the information activity.

Evaluating

From simple sentences to complicated grammatical structures and vocabulary, all students can give an opinion. The important thing is to make sure their opinion is well formed. This is where evaluating comes into play. It can help students make judgements about information, opinions, and items. It is used to form judgements that are sound and based in logic. This leads to more complex usage of language and the development of more intricate sentence structures.

A good way to introduce evaluating into language practice is to have students assess the validity of an opinion/information. When a student hears or reads an opinion or some information in a textbook, it is important to encourage them to ask questions about it. Where did the information come from? Is it factually correct? Does it stand up to the norms of the student's home culture? With the aforementioned activities in mind, you can ask students to start making their own opinions about information presented to them in a textbook and from the research they do on their own. In addition to the forming of opinions, it is just as important to require students to justify their answers with the information they found from the research.

Creating

Finally, we come to the act of creating. The highest tier of the HOTS taxonomy, creative thinking is essential for getting students curious and using English in situations not covered in a textbook. Creation is beneficial for mental flexibility, originality in producing language, and making critiques on what students read and hear. These abilities are core to developing fluency and spontaneity in academic and everyday interactions.

Teachers can bring students into creation in language activities by expanding topics into active learning opportunities. By taking a textbook's topic further and expanding on the initial setting or information, students can use real-world problems to acquire new knowledge. By creating solutions to problems, advice for friends, and even recipes for food, students are engaging in the act of creation. These activities can be further expanded into critical thinking activities by having students analyze shared recipes, research substitutions for advice, or justify the solutions they create (using facts and information found in research).

Conclusion

As you can most likely see, many of the higher-order skill activities tend to build upon one another. This is because each step in the hierarchy depends on the lower rungs of knowledge. These skills then form the foundation of critical thinking and encourage students to participate in intellectual pursuits to further their language acquisition experience. These types of activities can help students in developing fluency and achieving higher test scores (Dunn, 2016; Parrish & Johnson, 2010; Wong, 2016). All students, regardless of home culture, have the innate talent to utilize Critical Thinking Skills. These skills have the ability to impact almost every aspect of a student's life, from job hunting to gaining promotions and even making friends. By integrating higher-order thinking skills into language practice, educators can have an impact on a student's life even outside of the classroom.

References and Further Reading

Dalton, D. F. (2011, December). An investigation of an approach to teaching critical reading to native Arabic-speaking students. *Arab World English Journal, 2*(4), 58-87.

Dunn, J. (2016). The Effects of Metacognition on Reading Comprehension Tests in an Intermediate Reading and Writing Course. *OnCUE Journal*, 9(4), 329-343.

Finnish National Board of Education (2004). *National core curriculum for basic education*. Retrieved from http://www.oph.fi/english/sources_of_information/core_curricula_and_qualification_requirements/basic_education

Ford, C. L. & Yore, L. D. (2012). Toward convergence of metacognition, reflection, and critical thinking: Illustrations from natural and social sciences teacher education and classroom practice. In A. Zohar & J. Dori (Eds.), *Metacognition in science education: Trends in current research* (pp. 251-271). Dordrecht, The Netherlands: Springer.

Krathwohl, D. R. (2002). A revision of Bloom's taxonomy: An overview. Theory into Practice, 41(4), 212-218.

Moore, T. (2013). Critical thinking: seven definitions in search of a concept. *Studies in Higher Education, 38*(4), 506-522.

Mulnix, J. W. (2012). Thinking critically about critical thinking. *Educational Philosophy and Theory, 44*(5), 464-479.

Parrish, B., & Johnson, K. (2010, April). Promoting learner transitions to post-secondary education and work: Developing academic readiness from the beginning. *CAELA*.

Scriven, M. & Paul, R. (2007). *Defining critical thinking*. Retrieved from http://www.criticalthinking.org/aboutCT/define_critical_thinking.cfm.

van Gelder, T. (2005). Teaching critical thinking: Some lessons from cognitive science. *College teaching, 53*(1), 41-48.

Wong, B. L. (2016). Using Critical-Thinking Strategies to Develop Academic Reading Skills Among Saudi LEP Students

Q TIPS
Critical Thinking tips for Q Third Edition

As you start getting into *Q: Skills for Success*, you will find that higher-order thinking skills and opportunities for students to utilize critical thinking are well integrated into each unit. While it would be completely possible to use only the book (and the online activities) to improve a student's ability to utilize critical thinking, some educators may look to expand activities and get students to look deeper into the subjects introduced in the text. Below are three suggestions for expanding activities in the Student Book that will help you get the most out of it and your students.

1 Change the terms of an activity

When doing an activity, it can be beneficial for your students to tweak the parameters of an activity. *Q: Skills for Success* comes with excellent activities that utilize higher-order thinking skills to promote critical thinking. An example of this could be an activity that asks students to categorize information, for example, categorizing family members by age. The categorization metric, "age," could be changed to something else entirely.

Change the metric: Have students categorize family members by height, employment, or even how much they like each family member. This encourages mental flexibility and primes the student for creative use of English.

Get the students involved: Ask students to come up with new ways to approach the activity and use these ideas to expand on the topic, vocabulary, and skills they can practice.

2 Get online

Twenty-first century skills have come to the forefront of the educational mindset. Giving students the opportunity to go online, use English, and even go beyond the Student Book is important for utilizing skills that students may need to be a global citizen. *Q: Skills for Success* comes with a host of online practice that utilizes and expands the topics, vocabulary, and grammar in the textbook.

A jumping-off point: Educators can push students even further into online research and expansion of the learning topic. Have them investigate aspects of a topic they find interesting.

The class consensus: After students do their own research, have them share their findings with the class and write them on the board. After everyone has shared, you can discuss the results from a whole-class perspective.

3 Expand into deeper critical thinking skills

Q: Skills for Success Third Edition has an array of first-rate critical thinking and higher-order thinking skills built into each unit with activities in the Student Book and in the Online Practice. Once the activity is finished, you can further move the class toward critical thinking skills by having students share their answers, ask questions about how they came to those answers, and justify their answers to each other.

Give students the chance to compare and contrast: By giving students the opportunity to share answers with each other and compare their findings, you allow them to brainstorm new ideas, evaluate each other's answers, and develop debate skills naturally.

Justify justify justify: Whenever you have your students give an opinion, make sure they are justifying their opinions with evidence, life experience, or both. Circular logic like "I like pizza because it is delicious, and it tastes good." is something that needs to be avoided. A better answer would use their life experience to justify their like of pizza such as, "I like pizza because it is delicious. Tomato sauce is so great and even a little healthy!" Strive to have students give good opinions at all times.

Making Assessment Effective
Elaine Boyd Q Series Consultant, Assessment

In most educational settings nowadays, the requirement for assessments, both classroom and summative at the end of a course, is increasing. Teachers regularly assess their students informally in class, but they often get very little support or training in what and how to assess in a more structured way so that the tests are valid for learning and give reliable information to the teacher. Teachers intuitively understand that any assessment needs to be fair—both in terms of what is expected of the students and in the results that reflect the students' ability or competence in language. A learning program should include ongoing assessments that feed back into the classroom, give students information about what they need to focus on, and allow teachers to plan class content according to their students' needs. This is commonly known as Assessment for Learning and, although these assessments are usually conducted informally in class, they still need to be designed and delivered in a way that is fair and valid if the tests are to support learning effectively. What can help teachers to both manage and deliver fair and meaningful assessments that progress learning is an understanding of the principles that underlie assessment, why these principles are important, and how to make sure any assessment aligns with the principles.

The main points to consider when implementing an assessment program is the purpose of the assessment, its suitability for the intended test-takers (i.e. the students), and the reliability of the results. We capture these by implementing three principles—validity, reliability, and fairness/fitness for purpose. Let's consider each in turn.

Testing principle 1: Validity

We say a test is valid when we know it is testing what we intend it to test and that the testing focus (or construct) aligns with what the test-takers needs are. Put simply, this means you need to have a very clear idea of what construct (or sub-skill/competence) you are testing. For example, if we want to test a speaking skill, we don't set a task that involves a lot of reading because we will not know if the student has given a poor performance because of a lack of competence in reading or in speaking. Equally, if we want to assess a student's discourse competence, such as the internal organization of a piece of writing, then we need to give them a task that gives the test-taker a good opportunity to demonstrate this. Each test task needs to have a tight focus on what it is testing and not aim to assess too many things at the same time. This is why tests often have a variety of task and item types. This is arguably the most important principle, and if a test is not valid, it will never be reliable or fair.

Testing principle 2: Reliability

Reliability is very important for major summative tests, which can be very high stakes in that they can have a life-changing outcome. But many teachers do not realize that reliability is important even for classroom tests. We need to be sure that the information we are getting about the students' learning or achievement is correct because actions ensue from these results. This means even for informal classroom and ongoing assessments, we need to aim to make any assessment reliable. We do this by making sure the instructions are clear, that the tests are standardized so that even different versions are testing the same skills or competences, the marking is standardized, students are only tested on what they have been taught, etc. This can be a particularly challenging issue when we think about productive skills, which are core to communicative competence, but it is important to be as consistent as possible so that our students feel that they have been fairly assessed.

Testing principle 3: Fairness

In many ways, fairness is what drives the need for valid and reliable tests, but there is another aspect to fairness that can make a real difference to the test-taker and that is their involvement in the process. This involvement includes communication with students about what is expected of them and why, ensuring they are aware of what they will be assessed on, e.g. performance criteria of grading scales, and always giving meaningful feedback regarding the results of the assessment. This is especially important in ongoing classroom assessment models.

Effective feedback

Arguably the whole purpose of an ongoing classroom assessment program is to generate feedback, which will help both the students and the teacher. It is important for students to understand both what they have been successful at, as well as where they could improve. At the same time, classroom assessment also generates feedback for teachers so they can understand where they may need to implement a remedial or alternative approach to the learning objectives. Research evidence indicates that feedback works best (a) when it is given as soon as possible, (b) when only one or two points are targeted for improvement, and (c) where good guidance is given to learners on how they can improve, i.e. the specific action they need to take to help them. Remember all the tests have an extended answer key which explains why one answer is correct and others are not. This is to support teachers with any explanations and for students who may wish to reflect on any incorrect answers.

References and Further Reading

Bachman, L. & Palmer, A. (2010). *Language Assessment in Practice*. Oxford: OUP.

Fulcher, G. (2010). *Practical Language Testing*. London: Routledge.

Wall, D. (2012). *Washback*. London: Routledge.

TIPS
Assessment tips for Q Third Edition

1 **Make sure students know what is expected of them**

Before starting any test, discuss with students what they will be assessed on. This might be a skill or a vocabulary set or a range of language features.

Students need to know how they are being assessed, so go through the rubrics for Writing or Speaking (this will be one or the other – Writing for *Reading and Writing*; Speaking for *Listening and Speaking*) with them to make sure they understand the different assessment criteria and how these link to their learning.

2 **Give feedback as soon as possible after the test**

Discuss or point out what students have done well and then give them, either individually or as a class, a single point to improve. Discuss ideas with them around how they might improve but make sure you also have some suggestions to support them.

3 **Use the student reflection worksheet**

Make sure students understand each question in the worksheet; then allow them to complete it individually. Students can then discuss their answers in pairs, groups, or as a whole class. You can vary this throughout the course so everyone can share ideas. It's a good idea to build up a list of options for Questions 4 and 5 that everyone can have access to.

4 **Use the expanded answer key effectively**

The answers can either be discussed with the class or you may wish to ask students to do their own analysis first and then check how close their understanding is. If, after checking, students are still unsure of why an answer is incorrect, use the expanded key to discuss as a class and/or to prepare any remedial activities.

ASSESSMENT

Did you know that approximately 300 hours of video are uploaded to YouTube every minute? From clips of popular TV shows to music videos to online talks, there is a seemingly infinite variety of videos out there for teachers and students to use as language learning resources.

In fact, there is so much out there, it can actually feel a bit overwhelming. It's incredibly time-consuming to weed out the videos that aren't appropriate or aren't at the right level. Once educators find a video for use, we have to figure out how to transform it from a passive activity to an opportunity for language learning. But creating a worthwhile activity that matches the learning outcomes for the lesson and pushes students to produce language takes time, something today's educators have precious little of.

So before we dive down the YouTube rabbit hole, it's important to keep in mind the reasons why we use videos in our English lessons and how we can save time by taking advantage of videos already tailored to our lessons.

The Benefits of Using Video in Language Learning

First, videos provide an excellent scaffold for academic topics. The visual support they provide can give students access to content that otherwise might be beyond them. For instance, if students are learning about the laws of science, as they do in *Q: Skills for Success Third Edition, Listening and Speaking Level 4*, watching a video on Moore's law can help students understand better what they are hearing.

In addition, students of all ages genuinely enjoy watching videos. Watching TV is a popular activity for relaxation around the world, so learners tend to associate it with positive emotions. Neuroscientists assert that positive emotions tag learning events and give them prominence in the memory. What this means is that there is actually a biological purpose for making language learning fun, and using videos is one way to achieve that goal.

Finally, videos are an increasingly common source of information in the world nowadays. Where people used to get their news and information from articles and books, now they might also search for video clips on a topic as well. So exposure to video and incorporating them into teaching regularly is a useful 21st-century skill. However, as alternative sources for information have flourished, the need for students to become skeptical consumers has also grown. Critical thinking skills, therefore, are an important part of learning from videos.

Using Authentic Videos

The internet is crammed with all kinds of videos. But which ones will best meet the needs of our learners? Most teachers would probably agree that using authentic videos, in other words, content that was created with a purpose other than language learning in mind, grabs the attention of students and can motivate them and challenge them. The problem is that "real" videos are often very difficult for people who are not yet proficient users of a language to understand.

The most obvious solution to this problem is for teachers to turn to graded videos. For instance, beginning level students would probably be frustrated if they had to watch an American news report about the emotional benefits of running. The pace of the speaker would be too fast and the students probably wouldn't know much of the vocabulary. However, a graded video covers the same topic and the same content, but with vocabulary and grammar structures that are familiar to the learners and at a pace that is manageable. Luckily, teachers who use *Q: Skills for Success* can take advantage of the videos and accompanying activities presented in the Student Book and online. These videos come from authentic sources, though the language is often graded at lower levels to make the content accessible and level-appropriate.

Using Teaching Videos

The internet is chock-full of English teaching videos, too. There are lessons on everything from grammar points to conversation strategies to pronunciation tips. Sometimes these skills videos are great. Because the information is under the control of the students, they can watch them again and again and even use them to review for quizzes or brush up on their skills. Certainly, these videos allow students a certain degree of autonomy over their learning.

However, it can take a while to find videos that are relevant to the lesson. Unfortunately, not all the skills videos out there are accurate or of a high-quality. Sharing skills videos such as these with learners requires a teacher to spend time searching for videos that are a good match for the students and the lesson, are well-made, and (most importantly) are actually correct.

Again, *Q: Skills for Success* comes to the rescue. The skills videos that accompany each unit are professional quality, level-appropriate, and reliable. These videos can be used to introduce new concepts, provide additional support for struggling students, and allow opportunities for review.

Using videos in language learning is certainly fun, but it's not just fun. Videos can help students learn more easily and remember more. Although it can require a time commitment from teachers (unless you are using the *Q* videos, of course), most students would agree that it's time well spent!

Q TIPS
Video tips for Q Third Edition

1 Prepare
Using a video in class involves a lot more than just playing it. After all, the key is to make the video more than just the video; there always has to be a pedagogical purpose to everything we do in the classroom. So it's important for teachers to plan follow-up activities, such as answering comprehension questions, defining new vocabulary, writing sentences, or completing a T-chart. *Q: Skills for Success* offers scaffolded activities like this that have been created with your learners in mind; however, you can always include a few more activities if your students find a topic particularly engaging.

2 It's not just for listening
Consider using videos for more than just listening comprehension. You can integrate video expansion activities into every skill area—reading, writing, listening, speaking, grammar, vocabulary, and pronunciation! The *Q: Skills for Success Teaching Notes* contain many out-of-the-box ideas for squeezing every last drop out of a video clip. You might be surprised to learn all the different ways to use videos in the language classroom that go far beyond the traditional fill-in-the-blank activity.

3 Use the transcript
When possible and appropriate, make sure students have the opportunity to read the transcript as they watch a video. The act of listening while reading is enormously helpful to English learners because it reinforces sound/spelling correspondence and helps weaker listeners develop bottom-up listening skills like segmenting speech into words.

4 Flip the classroom
Experiment with using videos to flip the classroom. Assign skill videos from *Q* or those developed by other teachers online as homework. Make students accountable for watching the video by giving them a handout that asks questions about things that appear in the video as well as about the skill itself. Then in class, set aside a little time to address questions before transitioning into interactive practice activities. Flipping the classroom reduces the amount of teacher talk time and increases the amount of time that students have for producing the language. As well, struggling students can watch the skill video again and again until they understand, as opposed to having one chance at hearing the information in a teacher's lecture in class. It's a win-win!

To go online or not to go online?
Chantal Hemmi

Chantal Hemmi suggests a hermeneutical process to finding out about student progress and future needs.

A hermeneutical process is all about being a good listener and observer of student progress over time: 'Essentially, hermeneutics accords an important role to the actors and demands sensitivity and ability to listen closely to them' (Young and Collin, 1988:154).

With increasing learner access to both authentic materials as well as materials written for language learners online, teachers are faced with a question: Shall I go online in class or not? The same goes for homework. One way to make this informed choice is for teachers to think critically about the aim of the lesson. Here are some questions we could ask ourselves:

- Will the activity raise interest in the new topic area?
  Is it more effective to go online to stimulate interest in the subject, or do we want in-class activities that incorporate an interactive, kinesthetic element with the use of cue cards or pictures to encourage students to brainstorm activities interactively?

- Do we want to go online to do a reading or listening exercise, or a vocabulary learning activity for input? Can this be done more effectively online, or are your students in need of more face-to-face scaffolding of content and language before you go online?

- Are we encouraging students to develop their autonomy by going online to do some research on an essay or presentation topic? Do the students have access to a library from which to borrow books or download reliable materials? Which is the better option for them, to go online or to use paper-based publications, such as books?

The choice must always link into the aims of our courses. We have to bear in mind the strategy we want to take in order to develop students' knowledge of the content, the language they need to function in the class, and also the opportunity for students to think critically about what they are learning. Teachers must decide what mode of input and output we want in order to scaffold the content, language and skills students need to deal with communication in our diverse global communities.

How do good teachers that I know find out about what is authentic to the learners? Some go for needs analysis questionnaires. Others opt for interviewing or focus groups where you set a list of semi-structured open-ended interview questions that you want the learners to discuss.

In my view, teaching itself is a hermeneutical process of finding out about where the students are with their learning, what they have learnt and what they are still not confident about, and how they want to get the input, online or through basic scaffolding through classroom interaction, with the teacher facilitating the construction of new knowledge or language input. Not only should we be a good listener and observer, but also we should have the ability to choose tasks that best fit the class learner profile, based on our observations about where they are with their learning.

Thus, a hermeneutical process of finding out about student progress and future needs does not only look at snapshots of learners at a point in time, but looks at what happens over a term, or over the whole academic year. For example, a short speaking or writing test taken before mid-term can show a snapshot of the student's ability at that point in time. But we can include different modes of assessment such as group interviews, presentations, and essay-writing tests to see what kind of progress is observed over time. The key to making the process hermeneutical is to construct a dialogue through online or paper-based learner diaries so that students can reflect on their progress and about what they are learning. The teacher can make comments about student observations and thus sustain the dialogue over a period of time.

BLENDED LEARNING

I myself learnt through experience that when I am still being controlled by the actual technology, blended learning cannot help to manifest the aims of the course. The beauty of an effective blended learning journey will only be actualized when the teacher gains control over the technical as well as the methodological knowledge and skills to design courses so that in every lesson, the teacher knows why he/she is going online or choosing to stay with face-to-face input. Blended learning is a site of struggle, because the teacher has to question his/her role and to become skilled in making those important decisions that are going to play a crucial role in the design of our courses. Ultimately the aim is to conduct activities that benefit our learners with varying needs. Finally, blended learning also gives the teacher and students opportunities to explore effective modes of learning and to make the learning experience authentic to the learner.

References and Further Reading

Garrison, D. & Kanuka, H. Blended learning: Uncovering its transformative potential in higher education. *The Internet and Higher Education* 7 (2), 2nd Quarter 2004, 95-105. (http://www.sciencedirect.com/science/journal/10967516)

Young, R. & Collin, A. (1988). Career development and hermeneutical inquiry. Part I : The framework of a hermeneutical approach. *Canadian Journal of Counselling* 22 (3), 153-161.

Walker, A. White, G. (2013). *Technology Enhanced Language Learning* Oxford: Oxford University Press.

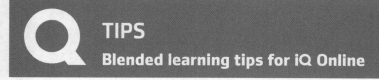

TIPS
Blended learning tips for iQ Online

1 **Always think what your end product is going to be at the end of a unit**
What do your students need to be able to do at the end? What kind of content, language and skills input do they need to be able to reach that goal?

2 **To go online or not to go online, that is the question!**
At the start of the unit, students have the opportunity to discuss the unit question online. Ask whether it is the right time to take the students to the Online Discussion Board or not. Have the students already got a rapport with each other to work collaboratively face to face? If so, this might be a good time to do some learner training to demonstrate how the Online Discussion Board works.

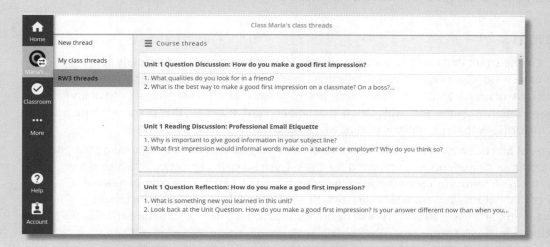

3 **Reading an online article: applying the study skills learnt off line**
Go online to guide students to preview the vocabulary, read the paragraphs and do Quick Write. This is a good way to encourage students to interact with the text online. The reading exercises present examples of sentence structures and vocabulary needed to do the final writing task. This is a nice way to integrate the reading and writing activity.

4 **The end product: the writing assignment**
At the final writing stage, a writing model is presented to scaffold the shape of the writing task. This is followed by graphic organizers that show the structure of the paragraph, and grammar exercises online.

Students plan and write the assignment online. After writing, there is a peer review exercise that could be done. If my students need practice in writing offline, in handwriting, I might ask the students to do so without going online.

BLENDED LEARNING

Using Communicative Grammar Activities Successfully in the Language Classroom

Nancy Schoenfeld

Have you ever tried to use a communicative grammar activity in class only to have it flop? Have you ever stood helplessly by as students look blankly at each other and then commence to talk with one another in their native languages? I have. It is an unpleasant feeling to watch your students have an unsuccessful experience in the language that they are trying to learn, especially when you chose the activity. I admit, too, that after such an experience I've thought that communicative activities just don't work.

Fortunately, I have discovered that communicative grammar activities DO work, that students enjoy them immensely, and they have an impact on language learning. Communicative activities in general encourage students to learn in creative and meaningful ways while promoting fluency (Richards & Rodgers, 2001). I have also discovered that HOW the language teacher executes the activity is just as important as the activity itself. I hope that these suggestions will help you as you plan to use communicative grammar activities in your own classrooms.

Sequencing

First of all, it is important that communicative grammar activities are positioned properly in the overall grammar lesson. (see Fig. 1). One mistake that I made was to have my students attempt to do a communicative grammar activity too soon. Ur (1988) suggests that there are four parts to grammar lessons: presentation, isolation and explanation, practice, and test. However, the "practice" step can be broken down further into three additional steps which build upon each other (Ur, 1988).

The first type of practice activities should be devoted only to the form of the grammar being taught. This gives a chance for students to understand the rules. The next type of practice activities allows students to focus on form plus the meaning of the grammar point. Last are the communicative grammar activities which allow for freer expression by students while still utilizing the taught forms. As you can see, there is a lot of work to be orchestrated by the instructor before attempting these activities.

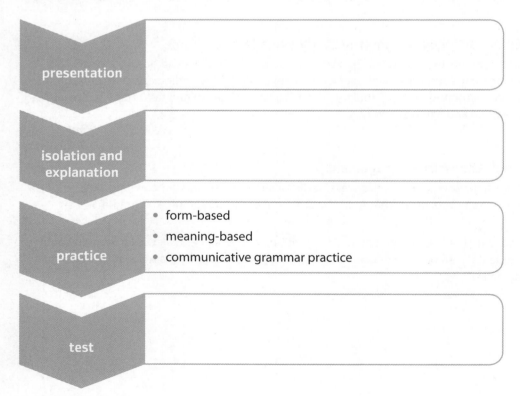

presentation

isolation and explanation

practice
- form-based
- meaning-based
- communicative grammar practice

test

Fig. 1 Sequencing grammar lessons (Ur, 1988)

Modeling

Before launching into a communicative activity, it is important to **model** the activity properly. It is not enough to merely *tell* your students what to do, you need to *show* them how to execute the task. For example, if the task is to practice question forms and I've given my students a list of questions to ask three other students, and a place to take notes, I would model the activity by having a student join me up in front of the class while I ask him some of the questions and record the answers. Then I ask another student to join me and so forth.

It is also important to show your students what they *aren't* supposed to do. To use the above example, it is tempting for students to form a group of four students with one person answering the questions and the three others recording the answers. This severely limits the amount of language practice the activity was designed for. And if you don't want students to look at each other's papers, such as in an information gap activity, mime holding your paper close to your chest so students understand that they are to talk and listen and not read.

Observing

During the communicative grammar activity, it is important to circulate around the room. The purpose for this is two-fold. First, you want to make sure that all students are participating fully in the activity and that they are not facing any difficulties. Sometimes students are stuck on the meaning of a word and this is preventing them from completing the activity. Your attentiveness can help them get unstuck and proceed. It is also a good opportunity to listen in on how students are using the grammar being practiced. If you hear a lot of errors, note them down and address them when the activity has finished.

Being persistent

Finally, it is important to not give up if your first forays with communicative grammar activities are not as successful as you hoped. Our students come from a variety of educational backgrounds. If they have had negative English language learning experiences, they bring those instances with them into our classrooms. Some students may be reticent to speak because errors brought punishment, belittlement or embarrassment. Others may have just been conditioned to take high-stakes language exams and have had little opportunity to actually communicate in English. In his excellent book on student motivation, Dörnyei (2001) describes different strategies that teachers can utilize to overcome these difficulties. These include making sure that language tasks can be completed successfully by students, that the activities themselves are fun and relevant, and that the teacher makes the classroom environment as comfortable as possible for students.

I will never forget the first time I conducted a successful communicative grammar practice activity. The classroom atmosphere changed completely. My students were smiling and laughing, grateful for a chance to move around and actively communicate with each other instead of just being passive listeners. I was thrilled because they were getting vital practice in an enjoyable and meaningful way. I was also pleased with myself because I hadn't quit trying to make this moment possible. Yes, successful communicative grammar activities require a lot of thought and planning on the part of the teacher, but the dividends are gold. May you and your students experience many of these golden moments.

References and Further Reading

Dörnyei, Z. 2001. *Motivational Strategies in the Language Classroom*. Cambridge: Cambridge University Press.

Jacobi, M. 2010. *Grammar Practice*. Brattleboro, Vermont: Pro Lingua Associates.

Lewis, M. & Hill, J. 1985. *Practical Techniques*. Independence, Kentucky: Cengage Learning.

Richards, J. & Rodgers, T. (2001). *Approaches and methods in language teaching*. Cambridge: Cambridge University Press.

Ur, P. (1988). *Grammar practice activities*. Cambridge: Cambridge University Press.

The practice stage of a grammar lesson has three distinctive parts: form-based practice, meaning-based practice, and communicative activities. Here are examples of all three types of practice activities focusing on conjunctions.

1 Form-based practice

Students practice when and when not to use commas while using conjunctions. The conjunction is provided for students so they don't need to worry about the meanings of conjunctions at this stage.

Directions: Insert a comma where necessary.

1. I like to eat chicken but not fish.
2. I lost my credit card so I need to get another one.
3. We will visit Paris and then we will fly to London.
4. Do you want tea or coffee?

2 Meaning-based practice

This next practice activity requires students to add the correct conjunction according to the meaning of the sentence.

Directions: Add *and, but, or* or *so* to the following sentences. Add a comma if necessary.

1. They were hungry _____ they ordered some pizza.
2. Do you want to go out for breakfast _____ lunch?
3. I have six brothers _____ sisters in my family.
4. I like this bag _____ it is too expensive. I can't buy it.

3 Communicative activity

A communicative activity allows for freer communication while still practicing conjunctions. Each student will have different answers which makes the activity interesting.

Directions: Ask 5 students the following questions. Students should use *and, but, or* or *so* and complete sentences when answering.

1. What is your favorite food? What food do you not like?
2. What two places would you like to visit on your next holiday?
3. What are two things you usually do on weekends?
4. What reason do you give your teacher when you are late to class?

In *Q* Third Edition, each unit has a communicative grammar activity designed to give students freer and meaningful practice using the grammar introduced in the unit. You can download these Communicative Grammar Worksheets on iQ Online Practice.

Vocabulary in your students' writing: the Bottom Line

Cheryl Boyd Zimmerman Q Series Consultant, Vocabulary

Isn't it obvious? In order to write well, we need to know a lot of words, and we need to know a lot about each word so we can use it to say what we mean. In fact, without the knowledge of many words, our writing is stymied—or should I say *crimped*? *impeded*? *blocked*? *snookered*? A word choice transmits not only meaning, but tone and subtleties of meaning such as familiarity or distance, precision or vagueness, certainty or ambiguity, earnestness or light-heartedness and more. For academic writing, this becomes especially challenging. In order to communicate as I intend, I need to know the ways in which words vary and then I need a wide variety of words from which to make my choices.

Why isn't vocabulary development included in every writing class? Perhaps we underestimate the difficulty of this task and prefer to spend precious classroom time on other issues. Or perhaps we don't know how to integrate word learning into writing in a way that is relevant to the writing task. But by not spending time developing our students' vocabulary, we are hindering their writing development and academic success.

This article suggests some techniques that address vocabulary development at each stage of the writing process: pre-writing, drafting, revision and editing, and gives you the bottom line when it comes to explaining the role of vocabulary to your students.

Pre-writing

This is the stage in which we gather ideas, develop thoughts and analyze the writing task. First, what type of writing (genre) is to be used: Newspaper article? Persuasive essay? Summary? Blog? This helps sort through the topic, choose how to focus attention and be clear about purpose and audience. Next, focus on finding a topic and exploring it with a purpose in mind. Reading and writing go hand-in-hand. To help students with both genre identification and topic development, use high-interest readings to provide clear models and to spawn ideas.

A focus on vocabulary can illuminate the topic and guide the planning. Pre-writing activities with a lexical focus might include:

Brainstorming:

- Students read the writing prompt or a short passage about the topic, and identify 1–2 words that stand out as central to the topic. For each one, students generate as many related words in 5–10 minutes without censoring themselves.
- Pairs or small groups compare lists, and explain their choices, keeping the topic and genre in mind. Encourage students to share words and add to their lists.

Freewriting:

* Students write non-stop for 5–10 minutes about whatever comes to mind that might relate to the topic, again without censoring themselves. Next, students reread what they wrote and circle words that seem important to what they want to say. Include words that describe facts, important names, opinions and feelings. Include synonyms that are related words in different registers.
* Using these selected words, describe your plans to a partner.

Paragraph Analyses:

Select a paragraph that is written in the same genre or on the same topic as the assignment. Provide copies or project on a screen. Read together as a class, drawing attention to vocabulary with questions such as:

* Which everyday words are used here?
* Which academic words are used here? (See examples at **oxfordlearnersdictionaries.com/wordlists/opal**).
* Focus on one well-used word at a time; what is behind the author's choice of each word? Select another paragraph and repeat this activity. Pairs work together to answer the same questions as above. Compare answers.

Bottom Line for Your Students

Different types of writing use different types of words. Even very academic papers don't use a large number of academic words, but they use them effectively. Academic texts contain an average of 10% academic words (Coxhead, 2006).

Drafting Stage

In this stage, vocabulary activities can evolve from a focus on meaning to a refinement of meaning, always related to whom you are writing for and why you are writing.

* As your students begin their first draft, refer to the words they identified during prewriting. Organize the way these words relate to each other as they develop their first draft.
* Return to the source text for the assignment or other relevant articles on the same topic. Identify words that stand out to your students as interesting and important to the message. Use these words in the writing.

Bottom Line for Your Students

Word learning doesn't just mean to learn new words, but also to learn to have confidence to use words that you recognize but don't use often. Writing gives you a chance to use partially-known words and to build your knowledge of these words.

Revision Stage

The revision stage is a time to check that your students' writing responded to the prompt, and that it focused on the purpose and audience as intended. Examples of doing this with a focus on vocabulary include:

- Ask your students to re-read the prompt and then re-read their papers. Do they address the prompt? Are there any words in the prompt that can be added to their papers for the purpose of congruity?
- Read through the papers and look for vague words (*good*; *nice*; *very*). With purpose and topic in mind, change them to be more specific and clear.

Bottom Line for Your Students

A study of 178 university professors found that the greatest problem with the writing of non-native speakers in their classes was vocabulary. They said vocabulary (more than grammar) kept them from understanding the meaning. (Santos, 1988) Your word choices are very important.

Editing Stage

The editing stage can be used as a guided opportunity to check for details of word-use including subtleties of meaning, lexical variety, grammatical features, derivatives and collocations. With this stage, students work with a final or near-final draft. Guide students to read through all or part of the paper, *focusing on one task at a time*:

- Lexical variety: Did they over-use any words? Did they repeat the same word in the same sentence?
- Noun use: Check their accuracy: Are they plural? Singular? Countable? Uncountable?
- Verb use: Do they "agree" with the nouns in plurality? Check for verb completion. Do the verbs need to be followed by an object? Do they need a "that" clause?
- Academic word use: Underline each academic word used. Has the student used them correctly? (When in doubt, check a dictionary.) Do they have enough? Too many?

Bottom Line for Your Students

You may have been taught to focus on grammar when you edit your paper, but grammar and vocabulary often overlap. Take time to focus on individual words; do they say what you mean and say it accurately?

Writing instruction and word learning belong together. These are some examples of ways to engage vocabulary development in writing.

References and Further Reading

Coxhead, A. (2006). Essentials of teaching academic vocabulary. Boston: Houghton Mifflin.

Santos, T. (1988). Professors' reactions to the academic writing of nonnative-speaking students. *TESOL Quarterly 22* (1), 69-90.

Q TIPS
Vocabulary tips for Q Third Edition

1 Prioritize important words
Help students to focus on the words that are most useful for them to learn, and encourage them to use those words. *Q Third Edition* incorporates both the Oxford 3000 or the Oxford 5000 and the Oxford Phrasal Academic Lexicon (OPAL), corpus-based lists that identify the most useful words to know in a general and academic context.

2 Use model texts to draw attention to vocabulary
Before starting the writing task, project the writing model on screen. Read together as a class, drawing attention to vocabulary with questions such as:
- Which academic words are used here?
- For each OPAL word, suggest a less formal word that the author might have used. What did the OPAL word add?
- Which everyday words are used here? What do they add?

3 Use the vocabulary from the reading
Students will have been exposed to relevant vocabulary in the reading part of the unit. Ask them to go back and refer to the earlier reading texts and Quick Write, and circle important words that they want to use in the writing assignment.

4 Encourage awareness of academic vocabulary
Students can highlight OPAL vocabulary in their writing. During the editing stage, check the following:
- Are there too few academic words? Too many? Does each academic word mean what you intend?
- Collocations: Are words combined accurately?
- Lexical variety: Are any words over-used? Or are the same words repeated in the same sentence?

5 Use technology to motivate students
Students can practice vocabulary online. For example, the vocabulary activities on *iQ Online Practice* make for a good revision tool. Each word has an audio file for pronunciation. This helps with memorizing the new words.

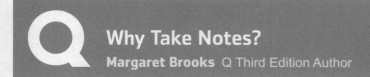

Q Why Take Notes?
Margaret Brooks Q Third Edition Author

Whether in the context of taking a phone message or listening to an academic lecture, note-taking is an essential skill for most language learners. In order to help learners acquire this skill, it is important to consider first the special challenges language learners face when trying to listen and take notes.

Short-term memory

One of the most self-evident issues is that it takes a language learner longer to process audio input than it does a native speaker. One reason for this is that a person's short-term memory is shorter in L2 than in L1. People employ short-term memory (usually measured in seconds) when processing audio materials. For example, when listening to a long sentence, the listener may need to hold the whole utterance in his/her mind and review it in order to comprehend it adequately. For the L1 listener this happens naturally, without the person being aware of it. However, for the language learner, this mental review process may not always be possible in the available time (Rost, 2005; Martin and Ellis, 2012).

Language structure

Another factor is the need for a mental map of the language, an internalized knowledge of the vocabulary and structures. A native speaker is grounded from childhood in the structures of the language and knows what to expect. We know, in fact, that people do not actually hear every word when they listen. But they hear enough to be able to parse out the meaning or reconstruct the sense quickly. They can "fill in the blanks" with words not actually heard.

Cultural expectations

Finally, in addition to being familiar with the semantic and syntactic aspects of the language, a listener may need to know of certain cultural expectations. Names of people and places and knowledge of events or history familiar to the average native speaker may be unfamiliar to the learner. All of these are things that may cause the listener to hesitate, stop listening, and try to think about what was said, while in the meantime the speaker continues. The listener then loses the thread and finds it difficult to bring attention back to the task.

How note-taking can help

In the face of these challenges, it may seem that adding note-taking to the listening tasks in the classroom may be a step too far for many. How, for example, can we expect high beginning students to listen and write at the same time? However, when the tasks are appropriate for the learners' level and carefully implemented, note-taking can actually improve comprehension.

Taking notes helps the student maintain focus and attention. It encourages a more engaged posture, such as sitting forward in the seat. The act of handwriting also aids in attention. Interestingly, studies have shown that students taking handwritten notes performed better on comprehension tests than those taking notes with an electronic medium such as a laptop or tablet. The reason for this is that handwriting is slower than typing. The writer has to summarize content, which involves more mental processing than faster typing. This in turn leads to better understanding and retention (Mueller and Oppenheimer, 2014).

The following are some examples of note-taking practice activities for the language classroom:

Preparing to listen

Although this is not a note-taking skill in itself, it is a necessary first step in the classroom. In real life, people do not usually approach something like a lecture or other listening context without some idea of what they will hear. They will have read assignments leading up to a lecture, received the agenda for a meeting, or at the very least know something about the topic.

We often put learners at an unfair disadvantage by starting a listening task by just saying, "OK, now listen to this." Pre-listening activities level the playing field by giving learners realistic preparation for the task. These can consist of things like pre-teaching key words, exploring students' prior knowledge of the topic, or short reading selections related to the topic.

Focusing on main ideas and key words

Some students have a tendency to equate note-taking with dictation and set out to try to write every word – something impossible even in L1. Activities that focus on writing only main ideas and key content words address this issue and help develop short-term, as well as long-term, memory. When students write down a few important words as they listen, seeing the words is a memory aid and helps them follow the flow of the ideas.

This strategy is essential when dealing with authentic listening texts at higher levels of language study and, by extension, in real-world situations. Authentic texts are likely to contain chunks of unfamiliar language that become "roadblocks" if students are not able to move past them and keep listening for key words.

Using a variety of organizational systems such as outlining, the Cornell Method, or even word webs

This enables students to follow the development of a speaker's ideas and "remember" them from start to finish as they listen. Presenting several ways of organizing notes shows that note-taking is essentially a personal task. Each person has to find a system that works for them.

Reviewing and adding to notes soon after a lecture or presentation

The purpose of note-taking in an academic setting is to provide students with a tool for study and review. In a business setting, notes from a meeting might be used to write a report or prepare a task list for a project. Notes consisting of just words and short phrases will not serve the purpose, as the note-taker will quickly forget how to put these together into a coherent record of a lecture or meeting, for example. In the classroom, students can review notes and expand what they have written. Also, even though there is no "rewind" function in a real-world lecture hall, it is useful practice for students to listen again and add to their notes.

NOTE-TAKING

Collaborating with others

Students often suffer from the mistaken notion that asking questions or getting help from others somehow diminishes them, makes them seem "stupid". They forget that even native speakers do this all the time and it probably comes naturally to them in their first language. In the classroom, students can compare notes with classmates, ask questions about things they didn't understand, and listen again to verify information.

Providing students with an opportunity to practice note-taking in a controlled and "safe" environment not only gives them a skill that will be useful in a variety of settings from the lecture hall to the meeting room, or even a doctor's office, but also helps them become more attentive listeners and improves general comprehension.

References and Further Reading

Martin, Katherine I and Nick Ellis (2012). The Roles of Phonological Short-term Memory and Working Memory in L2 Grammar and Vocabulary Learning. In *Studies in Second Language Acquisition*, Vol. 34, Issue 03, Cambridge University Press.

Mueller, Pam A and Daniel M. Oppenheimer (2014). The Pen is Mightier Than the Keyboard: Advantages of Longhand over Laptop Note Taking. In *Psychological Science*, Sage Journals.

Rost, Michael (2005). Research in Second Language Processes and Development. In Eli Hinkel (Ed). *Handbook of Research on Second Language Learning and Teaching*, Part IV. , Chapter 35: L2 Listening, Routledge.

Q TIPS

Note-taking tips for Q Third Edition

1 Foster a welcoming environment for critical thinking

Give attention to pre-listening activities. Teachers sometimes feel that this is "giving away" too much information and that the listening will not be a good "test" of students' skills. Remember that the listening tasks in *Q* are practice, not a test. Pre-teaching vocabulary and bringing out students' prior knowledge simply gives them tools that an L1 listener would bring to the task.

2 Acknowledge the adult learner's prior experience in academic settings

When presenting a strategy, ask if students have used a similar strategy in their L1 note-taking experience. For example, in Level 2 the note-taking strategy has students sketch plants for their notes. This is a quick way of recording information that would be difficult to put down in words. Ask if students ever use sketches in their L1 notes. For what subject matter would they be likely to do this?

3 Do as much as possible to lower stress levels as students listen

The controlled practice in each note-taking presentation in *Q* is an accessible activity designed to build confidence. For challenging material, you might want to "warm up" first. Tell students that you are going to play a portion of the recording and that you want them to tell you just one thing that they understood—even if it is only a few words. Play a short segment of the recording and then elicit answers from the class. This gives students a feeling of success and as they listen to their classmates' responses, they get more insight into the content of the listening.

4 Encourage students to use charts and other graphics to organize their notes

Elicit suggestions from students as to what type they might use. Does the listening describe a process? Then some kind of flow chart might be useful. Does it contrast two things such as pros and cons in an argument? Students might consider a T-chart.

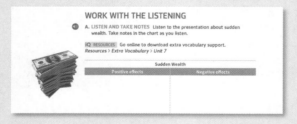

5 Provide feedback and follow-up activities after a listening

In real life, students often compare notes after a class. Many *Q* activities replicate this process in the classroom, asking students to compare notes with a partner, ask and answer questions about what they have heard, or add more information to their notes.

Q Academic Writing

Dr. Ann Snow Q Series consultant, Writing

Writing is a complex language form practiced by users of all languages (both native and non-native) for everyday social and communicative purposes and, for many, for vocational, educational, and professional needs. It has been variously described as a *product*—a piece of writing with a particular form and the expectation of "correctness." And as a *process*—a journey that takes writers through stages where they discover they have something to say and find their "voice." From the cognitive perspective, it is seen as a set of skills and knowledge that resides within the individual writer and from the sociocultural perspective as a socially and culturally situated set of literacy practices shared by a particular community (Weigle, 2014). With these perspectives in mind, all teachers of writing must ask: How can I help my students improve their writing and what are best practices in the classroom?

Needs assessment

An important first step is undertaking a needs assessment, whether informal or formal, to learn what kinds of writing students need. From this assessment, a syllabus or curriculum can be developed or a textbook series selected that is a good match with your students' needs. Typically, the instructional sequence starts with *personal/narrative* writing in which students have to describe or reflect on an experience or event. This usually leads to *expository* writing in which students learn to develop a thesis statement and support this controlling idea in the body of their writing. *Analytic* or *persuasive* writing is the most challenging type of academic writing because students must learn to state and defend a position or opinion using appropriate evidence (Ferris, 2009). These kinds of academic writing tasks require students to become familiar with a variety of text types and genres.

Improving vocabulary and grammar

The academic writing class also provides the opportunity for students to fine-tune their grammar and expand their academic language vocabulary. Typically, by the time our second language students are engaged in academic writing, they have been exposed to the majority of grammatical structures in English (e.g. complete tense system; complex constructions such as relative clauses and conditionals), but they still may need to learn how to integrate these structures into their writing. They also need to match text types with the kinds of grammatical structures needed. For example, in order to write a cause/effect essay, students need to use subordinating clauses with *because* and *since* and they need to use the appropriate transitional expressions like *therefore* and *as such*. Students will most likely have learned these structures in isolation but now need extensive practice and feedback to use them accurately in their writing. In terms of academic vocabulary, students need to differentiate the types of vocabulary found in everyday usage (e.g. the verbs *meet* and *get*) with their more formal academic counterparts *encounter* and *obtain* (see Zimmerman, 2009, for many other examples.)

In sum, the English for Academic Purposes curriculum must integrate reading and writing skills, and, as mentioned, grammar and vocabulary. Cumming (2006) points out that a focus on reading can lead to writing improvement and an opportunity to learn discipline-specific vocabulary. It also gives students something to write about. Combining reading and writing also provides needed practice in analyzing different text types so students see the features of these models. These kinds of activities create opportunities for more complex tasks such as summarizing and synthesizing multiple sources. A curriculum that integrates reading and writing also exposes students to graphic organizers for reading comprehension which students can recycle for pre-writing (Grabe, 2001). Finally, students need many exposures to similar tasks in order to master the complexities of academic writing and build confidence in their abilities.

References and Further Reading

Ferris, D. (2009). *Teaching college writing to diverse student populations*. Ann Arbor, MI: University of Michigan Press.

Grabe, W. (2001). Reading-writing relations: Theoretical perspectives and instructional practices. In D. Belcher & A. Hirvela, (Eds.), *Linking literacies: Perspectives on L2 reading-writing connections*. Ann Arbor, MI: University of Michigan Press.

Weigle, S. C. (2014). Considerations for teaching second language writing. In M. Celce-Murcia, D. M. Brinton, & M. A. Snow (Eds.), *Teaching English as a second or foreign language* (4th ed., pp. 222–237). Boston, MA: National Geographic Learning Heinle Cengage.

Zimmerman, C. (2009). *Work knowledge: A vocabulary teacher's handbook*. New York, NY: Oxford University Press.

TIPS
Academic writing tips for Q Third Edition

1 Use prewriting activities to generate ideas

Process approaches such as Quick Writes give students a chance to focus on their ideas for the unit assignment without being overly concerned with grammar, spelling, and punctuation at this early stage. You can then use open-ended questions to help students expand their ideas based on what they have learned in the readings and rethink and clarify their thinking before writing the unit assignment.

2 Model different kinds of texts

Students are shown the specific features of the text type required in the unit writing assignment (e.g. compare and contrast). Have students read and critique the model. Through the models, students develop awareness of the discourse features inherent in the kinds of writing required in each unit writing assignment.

3 Analyze good examples

Students learn to analyze different types of writing. For instance, they are provided with a list of features of a good summary, then they have to analyze and compare sample summaries and decide which samples best exemplify the features of a good summary.

4 Teach grammar in context

The grammar component tightly integrates the structure under focus with the text type of the unit. So, for example, students learn how to use the grammatical notions of parallel structure and ellipsis and then apply these to their unit writing.

5 Encourage strategic learning

Q encourages students to be strategic learners in all domains. Writing tips, for instance, guide students toward understanding the notion of unity in writing. Students learn that their thesis statements must be supported by details; doing so will create more coherence in their writing.

WRITING TIP

When you are freewriting, remember to write whatever ideas come to you. You can improve and revise your ideas later.

Using the Online Discussion Board

Notes and guidance on why and how to use the Online Discussion Board on *iQ Online Practice*.

Sigrun Biesenbach-Lucas, Ph.D., Senior Instructor
Donette Brantner-Artenie, M.A., Senior Instructor
Georgetown University, Center for Language Education and Development

Many students beginning their academic study today come to campus equipped with strong technology skills, yet they soon discover that they need to make the transition from experienced users of technology for social purposes to effective users of technology for academic purposes. Becoming familiar with and engaging in a variety of genres is part of academic study and is critical for both native (NS) and non-native English speaking (NNS) students. For NNS students, however, "learning to function in the genres and with the discourse conventions of their discourse communities poses a particular challenge" (Cheng, 2010, p. 74). Academic writing is one of the many discourse communities in which ESL students need to function and to follow specific conventions. While ESL programs have long prepared students for traditional academic writing assignments, like essays and research papers, formal online writing is often neglected in ESL instruction despite the growing need for such preparation.

Reasons for not including formal online writing assignments can range from limited resources, instructors' lack of confidence in their own technology skills, and questions about the relevance of this type of writing. A potential consequence of not addressing such writing is that NNS students may be less prepared for these types of assignments, which are becoming more common within hybrid classes, or blended learning contexts, or even in courses that are fully online. If ESL programs want to ensure that they prepare ESL students adequately for academic study, they need to consider ways to incorporate online writing components into their classes. In addition to serving as a "pathway to academic literacy development" (Cheng, 2010, p. 74) for

ESL students, online writing, through discussion boards or blogging tools, can offer them a greater variety of language learning opportunities to motivate autonomous language learning experiences. The same advances in technology that have afforded academic instructors with a variety of media that students use to demonstrate comprehension and applications of course content also need to be considered as additional tools for ESL teachers to use in their language teaching. The *Q: Skills for Success* series follows a blended learning approach that prepares students for future success and incorporates the benefits of online academic writing that are specific to language learning (**Fig. 1**).

Among online technologies, the discussion board is one of the easiest tools to use (TeacherStream, 2009), but students need to use the technology appropriately for formal online writing. Consequently, instructors need to make sure that they use this type of writing assignment effectively. More specifically, discussion board interactions should not involve informal or brief, undeveloped contributions resembling text messages or chats; rather, they should be carefully structured to generate well-supported, reflective ideas. "[A]lthough generally shorter and narrower in focus than a traditional essay, discussion posts should be as coherent and scholarly in tone [as essays]" (Discussion posts, 2014, para. 1). In this paper, we will first address the learning benefits associated with the use of discussion boards and then outline a structured approach to implementing discussion boards that maximizes their benefits and reinforces the idea that writing in online threaded discussions should be treated as a legitimate formal genre of academic writing.

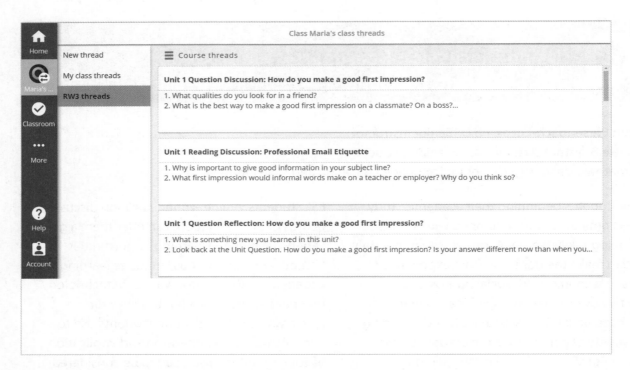

Fig. 1 *Q: Skills for Success* Third Edition, iQ Online Practice Class Discussion Board

Benefits

An examination of various sources that focus on the use of discussion boards with native speakers in educational settings (e.g., Blogs and discussion boards, 2014) shows that "the discussion board is the place where some of the most important learning can happen" (Generating and facilitating engaging and effective online discussions, n.d., p. 1), but only if implemented effectively. These types of posting activities typically include responses to and reflections on questions posed by the instructor or the textbook as well as replies to other students' posts. Some discussion board activities may also require students to integrate ideas from course materials (e.g., articles, lectures) or from their classmates' posts into their own posts.

Students in both content and language courses can benefit from discussion board writing activities. One outcome of these online tasks is that they prepare NNS students for future course work by developing their academic literacy skills (Cheng, 2010; Kingston, 2011) because a discussion board affords regular opportunities for students to practice their writing while following conventions for traditional types of academic writing, such as assignments with multi-paragraph structure, a main idea, and adequate support. At the same time, such regular practice

affords NNS students additional opportunities for language learning: teacher feedback provides added focus on grammar, vocabulary, and mechanics; classmates' reactions to language choices increase students' awareness of issues in their writing, such as lack of clarity and ambiguity.

Students also hone their critical thinking skills through discussion board writing, partly because of the asynchronous nature of the tool: students can take more time to reflect on their ideas or conduct research before they craft a post than they can in face-to-face classroom interaction (TeacherStream, 2009; Wijeyewardene, Patterson, & Collins, 2013). This deeper reflection usually results in more complex responses to the discussion board questions (Wijeyewardene, Patterson, & Collins, 2013) than are possible in oral discussions that take place in the classroom. Students who are shy, and therefore less likely to speak in class, can find a voice and take part in conversations online (Meloni, 2011). The confidence that students gain in online interactions can also transfer into the classroom.

Another outcome is that discussion board writing increases students' sense of audience. Because their writing is posted online, students are aware that their classmates can access and read their posts. This means that the typical classroom writing audience of one (i.e., the teacher) is expanded into an "authentic audience" (Blogs and discussion boards, 2014, para. 7) of many. Students are "exposed to a greater range and variety of interpretations of the topics they encounter in the course materials" (Goodfellow & Lea, 2005, p. 264). The heightened sense of audience and building of trust fosters a sense of learning community (Holland & Holland, 2014; Kingston, 2011; TeacherStream, 2009).

Considerations for the Teacher

Before implementing discussion board activities, teachers need to decide how and for what purposes these activities are going to be used. Traditionally, through their responses to questions posted by the instructor or through replies to specific classmates' posts, students can demonstrate authentic and meaningful use of language. Effective discussion board tasks require students to explain opinions and ideas clearly, to integrate their own ideas with those from other sources (including those of their classmates), to synthesize ideas from multiple sources, and to use appropriate language to react to other people's ideas. Through this process, instructors can guide students in demonstrating their knowledge of key concepts from class material, reflecting on and thinking critically about course topics, and working together to reach agreement on assigned topics (Lafford & Lafford, 2005; TeacherStream, 2009). Effective writing assignments in blended courses, both academic and ESL, seamlessly integrate discussion board writing prompts with the structure and content of the textbook or other class materials in one coherent framework. The authors of the *Q: Skills for Success* series follow this approach through their integration of the materials and activities in iQ, the online component of the series, and the Student Book.

Prior to implementation, instructors also need to assess the level of students' skill in using the online courseware that is available to them. To ensure that students approach the task with a clear understanding of the instructor's expectations, it is important for teachers to demonstrate to the class how to use the tool in an "orientation tutorial" (Wozniak & Silveira, 2004, p. 957) and allow the class to practice navigating the discussion board site before the

first formal assignment. Teachers should also have students explore model posts to discover the differences between discussion board writing and other forms of online communication with which students are more familiar (e.g., social media posts, text messages, email) (Generating and facilitating engaging and effective online discussions, n.d.).

Another consideration is the level of teacher participation in the posting activity. Based on students' level, instructors' choices can range from posting regularly—and, thus, serving as writing models for their students—to remaining an observer. However, at some point, all instructors need to shift from online participants who facilitate effective discussion board interactions to offline observers who monitor students' interactions (Online discussions for blended learning, 2009; TeacherStream, 2009) so that the class can learn to maintain effective communication that is independent of the teacher's guidance and modeling.

Since major goals of discussion board writing include developing critical thinking skills and reacting effectively and properly to the ideas of others, teachers should ensure that writing prompts contain questions that provide natural practice in these skills. Assigning a topic is not sufficient; good discussion board prompts encourage higher-order skills through *wh-*questions; questions that encourage students to reflect, interpret, analyze, or solve a problem; questions that draw out relevant personal opinion/experience; and questions that ask students to draw connections (Sample discussion board questions that work, n.d.). The materials in the *Q: Skills for Success* series, both the textbooks and the online supporting material, include such questions and allow instructors to pose their own questions/prompts based on these principles (**Fig. 2**).

Once teachers have decided which prompts to assign or which questions to post, they need to set expectations for and provide instruction in how to compose a quality post (Blogs and discussion boards, 2014; Boothon, 2012; Discussion posts, 2014; Goodfellow & Lea, 2005; Kingston, 2011; Online forums: Responding thoughtfully, n.d.; Wozniak & Silveira, 2004).

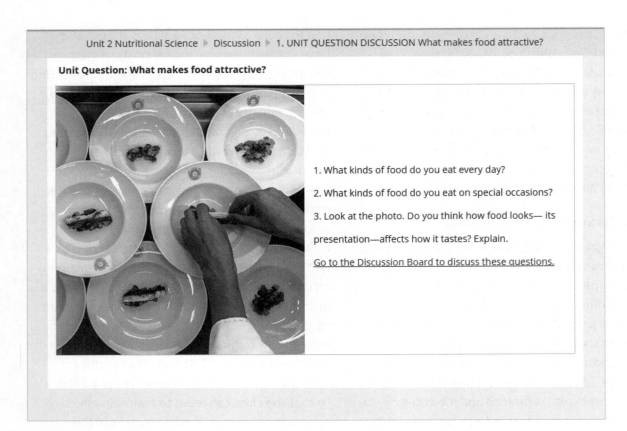

Unit Question: What makes food attractive?

1. What kinds of food do you eat every day?

2. What kinds of food do you eat on special occasions?

3. Look at the photo. Do you think how food looks— its presentation—affects how it tastes? Explain.

Go to the Discussion Board to discuss these questions.

Fig. 2 Examples of discussion questions from *Q: Skills for Success* Third Edition

Teachers should plan to address the following elements:

- requirements for participation and time parameters as well as expectations with respect to quality, length, and level of formality;

- a framework for composing well-developed paragraphs that address multiple questions, a format that tends to be characteristic of discussion board writing in academic courses; in ESL contexts, this framework should be designed to reflect the proficiency level of the students, progressing from the simple paragraph level to multiple integrated paragraphs;

- appropriate responses to classmates' posts that employ respectful and formal language, especially when there is disagreement about ideas;

- thoughtful responses to classmates' ideas that go beyond simple statements like "I agree with you," which are not constructive and do not promote further interaction among the students; responses that build on classmates' contributions and show critical thinking describe personal experiences, extend ideas to

other contexts, and/or support agreement or disagreement with sufficient examples; and

- effective incorporation of ideas from outside sources, such as class readings, lectures, and other material, and integration of ideas from multiple classmates' posts, especially when students are at higher levels of proficiency.

The discussion board activities in iQ gradually increase in complexity by level and require students to show increased skill in reflecting these elements of effective online writing.

In order for students to view discussion board writing as a legitimate academic genre and a relevant component of a course, it is critical that teachers provide routine, structured feedback (Blogs and discussion boards, 2014; Kingston, 2011; TeacherStream, 2009). One common approach to providing constructive feedback is through rubrics that assess quality, quantity, and language use as well as the observance of proper posting netiquette, which is defined as polite behavior for communicating online in a public forum. It is important that students become familiar with the writing criteria that their teacher will assess; in the iQ Discussion Board Teacher Pack, one of the reproducible worksheets is a discovery activity in which students apply a sample rubric to a model post. For the teacher's convenience, reproducible rubrics are also included in the iQ Discussion Board Teacher Pack. Once students are aware of the criteria in the rubrics, instructors can encourage them to use these rubrics as pre-submission checklists and for informal evaluations of their own writing.

Conclusions

When used effectively, discussion board activities offer NNS students a platform for "rehears[ing]" academic writing (Cheng, 2010, p. 74) and composing "thoughtful, constructive responses" to others' ideas, with which they may or may not agree. Students are likely to encounter the need for such language functions in future academic and professional contexts (Online forums: Responding thoughtfully, n.d., para. 7). Given that gaining proficiency this genre of writing poses specific challenges to language students, it is essential to implement online academic writing within ESL courses.

Regardless of the extent to which instructors incorporate discussion board writing with other required academic writing assignments, they need to guide students in establishing connections between their learning in the online environment and their face-to-face interactions in the classroom (Wozniak & Silveira, 2004). These connections ensure that ESL students understand that discussion boards are an important learning tool that they can employ and through which they can improve their academic language skills. For these reasons, discussion board writing activities are a valuable tool in ESL instruction.

Sigrun Biesenbach-Lucas received her M.A.T. and Ph.D. degrees in Applied Linguistics from Georgetown University. She has taught ESL, Linguistics, and teacher training courses, and she is currently teaching in the Intensive English Program at Georgetown University. She has also served as a site reviewer for CEA. She regularly presents at TESOL conferences; she has published articles in *Language Learning & Technology*, *Computer Assisted Language Learning*, and the *Journal of Asynchronous Learning Networks*, among others; and she is the co-author of the top level of a grammar textbook series that follows a blended approach.

Donette Brantner-Artenie holds an M.A. in Linguistics from Ohio University. She taught EFL in the U.S. Peace Corps in Romania and has conducted training programs for EFL teachers and teacher trainers overseas. In the U.S., she has taught ESL at Ohio University and Ohio State University, and she is currently teaching in the Intensive English Program at Georgetown University, where she also coordinates the program's labs. She is the co-author of the top level of a grammar textbook series that follows a blended approach.

References and Further Reading

Blogs and discussion boards. (2014). Vanderbilt University, Center for Teaching. Retrieved from http//cft.vanderbilt.edu/guides-sub-pages/blogs/.

Boothon, M. (2012). Tips for writing thoughtful discussion responses. Rasmussen College. Retrieved from http://www.rasmussen.edy/student=life/blogs/online-learning/tips-for-writing-thoughtful-discussion-responses/.

Cheng, R. (2010). Computer-mediated scaffolding in L2 students' academic literacy development. CALICO Journal, 28(1), 74–98.

Discussion posts. (2014). Walden University. Online Writing Center. Retrieved from http://writingcenter.eandenu.edu/1096.htm.

Generating and facilitating engaging and effective online discussions. (n.d.). University of Oregon Teaching Effectiveness Program.

Goodfellow, R., & Lea, M.R. (2005). Supporting writing assessment in online learning. Assessment & Evaluation in Higher Education, 30(3), 261–271. DOI: 10.1080/02602930500063835.

Holland, J., & Holland, J. (2014). Implications of shifting technology in education. TechTrends, 38(3), 16–25.

Kingston, L. (2011). Efficient and effective online discussion forums. Paper presented at the Assessment Teaching and Learning Conference 2011.

Lafford, P. A., & Lafford, B.A. (2005). CMC technologies for teaching foreign languages: What's on the horizon? CALICO Journal, 22(3), 679–709.

Meloni, J. (2011). Technologies for teaching: Strategies and pitfalls. The Education Digest, 76(8), 23–27.

Online discussions for blended learning. (2009). California State University, Sacramento. Academic Technology and Creative Services.

Online forums: Responding thoughtfully. (n.d.). Writing Commons. Retrieved from http://writingcommons.org/open-text/new-media/online-forums/651-online-forums-responding-thoughtfully.

Sample discussion board questions that work. (n.d.). McMurry University. Retrieved from http://www.mcm.edu/elearning/Tutorials/PDF/Discussion_Questions_That_Work.pdf.

TeacherStream. (2009). Mastering online discussion board facilitation: Resource guide. Retrieved from https://www.edutopia.org/pdfs/stw/edutopia-onlinelearning-mastering-online-discussion-board-facilitation.pdf.

Wijeyewardene, I., Patterson, H., & Collins, M. (2013). Against the odds: Teaching writing in an online environment. Journal of Academic Language & Learning, 7(2), A20–A34.

Wozniak, H., & Silveira, S. (2004). Online discussions: Promoting effective student to student interaction. Australiasian Society for Computers in Learning in Tertiary Education. Retrieved from http://www.ascilite.org.au/conferences/perth04/procs/pdf/wozniak.pdf.

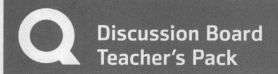

Teaching Notes

Objectives

A fundamental objective of a Discussion Board writing activity is for students to gain awareness of the conventions applied in the genre of online academic writing and to practice writing in this genre.

At the beginning of a unit, students use the Discussion Board activity to further activate prior knowledge about a new unit theme after discussing the initial Unit Questions and listening to *The Q Classroom* online. Students are again directed to the Discussion Board after the *iQ Online* Reading Comprehension activity in each unit to discuss the online text. At the end of a unit, the Discussion Board tasks provide opportunities for students to apply content knowledge, grammar structures and vocabulary, as well as writing strategies that they learned in the unit.

All the Discussion Board questions are designed to encourage critical thinking. Instructors can decide if they would like their students to respond to all of the given questions or select specific questions which they want their students to address. Additionally, instructors can post their own questions to which students respond.

Teacher's Pack Organization

Prior to introducing the Discussion Board to your students, it is necessary to familiarize yourself with the contents of the Discussion Board, the specifics of its navigation as well as deciding on an implementation strategy. These teaching notes discuss all three items.

In order to help you maximize the efficacy of the Discussion Board, additional resources have been provided. These will be referenced and explained within these teaching notes: grading rubrics, teacher navigation instructions, printable student navigation instructions ("Posting to the Discussion Board") and a student worksheet for classroom use ("Example Discussion Board Post").

Implementing the Discussion Board

Discussion Board Content

The Discussion Board contains three threads per unit. These threads are the Unit Question Discussion and the Unit Question Reflection. The Unit Question Discussion takes place at the beginning of the unit and contains a few questions to further the discussion of the Unit Question after completing *The Q Classroom* activities in the Student Book. Next is the Reading Discussion thread which accompanies the Reading Comprehension activity in *iQ Online*. This thread encourages students to engage with the topic of the online reading text. Finally, the Unit Question Reflection is provided at the end of the unit in order to reflect upon what the student has learned. In addition, the teacher may create new threads either by using the supplemental questions provided, the Challenge Questions, or any other question he or she deems appropriate.

Teaching Strategies

In terms of teaching strategies, the teacher must decide upon his or her level of involvement. You should decide if you want to participate in the online discussions or if you only want to read and evaluate your students' posts. If you post to the discussions, students can be encouraged by your engagement, but if you remain a reader, you can retain the focus on the students' writing and ideas.

In addition, it may be more suitable in Level 2 if the teacher is the only person to reply to students' posts in order to clarify ideas and guide students in writing effective responses. If appropriate, given the students' ability, the instructor may allow brief and structured responses to each other's posts. However, the teacher should structure the assignment to prevent students from posting one-word or very brief responses. This follow-up strategy can be used with all Discussion Board questions, both at the beginning and at the end of each unit.

For example, the teacher can refer to the example post on the student worksheet, "Example Discussion Board Post." In the example, the student wrote about his grandfather's positive attitude. A follow-up assignment in which students read and respond to a classmate can be structured as follows.

Read your classmates' posts. Write a reply to one person. In your reply, start the first sentence with "I would like to know more about …"

Potential student reply:
Jonathan, I would like to know more about your grandfather and his guitar lessons. He is 78 years old and learned how to play the guitar. I think that it is difficult for an older person to learn something new. My grandfather can't do something like that because he has pain in his hands.

Rubrics have been included to help grade the student posts and their replies to a classmate's post. It is important that students write an appropriate response that has complete sentences and uses formal language. This also means that the student's reply is directly connected to the ideas in the question or the classmate's post. It is important that students use the Discussion Board to express themselves, and do so in a way that is appropriate for the classroom context.

In addition to using the rubrics, assess the students' posts by printing them out or making electronic copies, and adding questions, comments, and other feedback. With students' permission, you can use good posts as models to illustrate strategies for effective writing. You can also collect language use examples from students' posts to illustrate grammar points and use these for group editing practice.

Classroom Instruction
Prior to First Post: Example Discussion Board Post Worksheet

This student worksheet, called "Example Discussion Board Post," provides an example of a discussion board post, which you can review with students to discover the structure and content of an effective post and to see how the instructor will apply the evaluation rubrics.

1. After talking in class about the Unit Question and the Unit Question Discussion questions, tell students that they will extend those ideas that they discussed in an assignment outside of class.

2. Distribute the student worksheet, "Example Discussion Board Post," to students. Tell them that they are going to learn how to write on a discussion board online and share information with their classmates and instructor when they are not in the classroom.

3. Review the example Unit Question Discussion. Start with the unit academic subject area, Psychology. Then review the Unit Question and the Unit Question Discussion questions with students. Clarify the meaning of "positive thinking." Point out that there are two additional questions that the students should address. Note that this is only an example unit and does not appear in the book.

4. Have students read the example post and answer worksheet questions 1 through 4. Have students compare their responses with a partner before checking answers with the whole class. If possible, project the post on the classroom screen, and highlight the relevant parts as you identify and discuss them with the class.

5. Review the discussion board rubric with students in task 5 of the worksheet. Have students apply the rubric to the example post and try to explain why they would give a certain rating in each category.

6. In the last task on the worksheet, the "Follow-up" task, have students brainstorm, in groups or pairs, ideas for responding to a new example question. Debrief with the whole class and check that students understand the process.

7. Review instructions on how to post to the Discussion Board. Use the page entitled

"Posting to the Discussion Board: Student Instructions." Follow up with a test post to ensure that all students know how to use the tool properly.

Assigning the First Discussion Board Post

1. Assign the first Unit Question Discussion response, and indicate the deadline for the post.

2. After all responses have been posted, have students read all of their classmates' posts.

Then in class, have students discuss the ideas in the posts to find commonalities and differences or to put ideas into possible categories.

3. Use the same process for the Reading Discussion and the Unit Question Reflection.

4. *Optional:* At the end of each unit, the teacher can assign one or both of the Challenge Questions. Follow the same process as for the other assignments. See complete list of Challenge Questions for all units.

Discussion Board Instructions

Before introducing this tool to your students, review "Posting to the Discussion Board: Student Instructions" to familiarize yourself with the online writing process. The student instructions are included in the student materials.

After completing the "Example Discussion Board Post" worksheet and reviewing the included rubric with your class, go over the student instructions with the students. If you have computer projection in the classroom, you may go online and demonstrate this process to the students.

Remind students that when they post to the Discussion Board, they need to make sure that they choose the correct Unit number and the correct question.

Logging in to the Discussion Board

1. Log in to iQ Online Practice.

2. Choose your class (under your level).

3. Choose Discussions.

Responding to a Classmate's Post

If you wish to participate in a Unit Discussion, you can follow the same instructions that the students use.

Creating a New Discussion Topic

All Unit Question Discussion and Unit Question Reflection questions are already on the Discussion Board site. However, if you want to assign Challenge Questions [refer to the included list of Challenge Questions], or if you want to pose questions of your own, follow these steps:

1. Choose New Thread.

2. In the subject line, write: "Unit X: Challenge Question 1," or "Unit X: (Your own writing topic)." Note: It is important that you identify the unit number as this will not be automatically added.

3. Copy and paste your selected Challenge Question, or type your own question, in the text box.

4. Click on Post.

Deleting a Post

As the instructor, only you have the ability to delete threads and individual replies, including entire Discussions. However, before you click Delete, be certain that you want to perform this action as it cannot be undone.

If you want to delete a single student post in a discussion or an individual response to someone else's post, go to that post, and choose the delete icon.

Suggestions for Using the Discussion Board Assignments

1. Good academic practice includes planning and carrying out online writing assignments offline first. By drafting and saving a post using a word-processing program, students can review and make changes to their writing before uploading the post. This practice also encourages another important academic skill, which is to keep a saved copy of one's writing.

2. Because your students cannot delete any posts from the Discussion Board themselves, they will need to contact you to delete a post for them if they made a mistake or posted to the wrong Discussion. Advise your students to follow whatever process you deem appropriate; for example, you can have students send you an email with a request to delete a post.

3. Review your students' posts regularly and in a timely fashion so that you can address issues as they develop or delete inappropriate posts.

Rubric: Response to Discussion Board Prompt

Name: _____   Date: _____

20 = Completely successful (at least 90% of the time).

15 = Mostly successful (at least 70% of the time).

10 = Partially successful (at least 50% of the time).

0 = Not successful.

Writing a Discussion Board Post	20 points	15 points	10 points	0 points
The post answers the question(s) clearly and completely.				
The post has clear and specific explanations and examples.				
The post shows careful thinking about the topic.				
Sentences are complete and have appropriate final punctuation.				
The post correctly includes vocabulary and grammar from the unit.				
The length of the post is appropriate.				
The post includes formal and polite language.				

Total points: _____ out of _____

Comments:

Rubric: Response to Classmate's Post

Name: _____ Date: _____

20 = Completely successful (at least 90% of the time).

15 = Mostly successful (at least 70% of the time).

10 = Partially successful (at least 50% of the time).

0 = Not successful.

Writing a Discussion Board Response	20 points	15 points	10 points	0 points
The response answers the question(s) clearly and completely.				
The response uses clear and specific ideas from the classmate's post.				
The response shows careful thinking about the classmate's ideas.				
Sentences are complete and have appropriate final punctuation.				
The post includes vocabulary and grammar structures from the unit.				
The response includes formal and polite language.				
The response is appropriately structured, positive opening statement and a closing sentence.				
The response includes one or more of the following: agreement/ disagreement/ example from personal experience.				

Total points: _____ out of _____

Comments:

Challenge Questions

You may choose to assign these Challenge Questions for students to respond to at the end of a unit. You will need to post the Challenge Question for each unit yourself as a new thread or threads.

Unit 1: Marketing

Unit Question: *Why does something become popular?*

1. In this unit, you read about "social proof," and how the behavior of others can influence our decisions to do something or to buy something. Currently, smart phones are very popular around the world. Which type or types of social proof have influenced you or someone you know to purchase a particular smart phone brand or type?

2. Select a product, and describe how you can create "buzz" about this product. What are some unusual or creative ways to make the product popular?

Unit 2: Psychology

Unit Question: *How do colors affect the way we feel?*

1. The basic color of Apple's iPhone was black. Later, the company added phones in white, gold, silver colors. Why do you think Apple chose those colors? What does Apple want its customers to feel?

2. Companies often create new names for the colors of their products. These names can be unusual or creative. For example, a blue car color can be "night sky blue", or a white shirt color can be "snowy day." Why do companies choose these new color names? How does this help them sell their products?

Unit 3: Social Psychology

Unit Question: *What does it mean to be polite?*

1. In this unit, you learned about culture and politeness. How do you show politeness with someone who is younger or older than you? What are some differences?

2. Around the world, cultural differences in the way people show politeness can cause problems. Do you think that there should be a set of "international good manners" that everyone uses? Why or why not?

Unit 4: Technology

Unit Question: *How can technology improve performance?*

1. In this unit, you read about how technology can improve an athlete's performance. However, some people think that using technology in sports creates an unfair advantage. What are some other situations where technology could create an unfair advantage? Why?

2. Can technology ever hurt someone's performance? When might technology make it more difficult to do something? Explain your answer.

Unit 5: Business

Unit Question: *What makes a family business successful?*

1. Some family businesses are over 100 years old. Why do you think these companies are successful? What do these businesses do that other family businesses do not do?

2. In a successful family business, what kind of skills should each family member have? Should everybody have a college degree, or work experience? How important are each family member's skills?

Unit 6: Brain Science

Unit Question: *How can you learn faster and better?*

1. Is learning faster always better? When would it be important to slow down the learning process? Why?

2. What do successful students have in common? Could these common characteristics help unsuccessful students learn faster and better? Explain.

Unit 7: Environmental Science

Unit Question: *Do cities need nature?*

1. What would it be like to live in a city without any parks or natural spaces? How would the lack of nature affect people living there?

2. Describe the best park or natural space you have ever been to in a city. What makes this place special?

Unit 8: Public Health

Unit Question: *How can we prevent diseases?*

1. Every year, we hear about new illnesses that can spread quickly from person to person, and even around the world. What do you do when you hear about a new illness? How do you stay healthy?

2. In this unit, you read about how doctors are working to treat and prevent diseases such as Ebola and malaria. What are some other major diseases that doctors should focus on? Which disease should be the top priority? Why?

Unit Specific Notes

Unit 1: Marketing

Challenge Questions 1 and 2

1. *In this unit, you read about "social proof," and how the behavior of others can influence our decisions to do something or to buy something. Currently, smart phones are very popular around the world. Which type or types of social proof have influenced you or someone you know to purchase a particular smart phone brand or type?*

2. *Select a product, and describe how you can create "buzz" about this product. What are some unusual or creative ways to make the product popular?*

Review with students the meaning of "social proof" and ensure that students understand the word "buzz" in the advertising context.

Unit 2: Psychology

Challenge Question

Companies often create new names for the colors of their products. These names can be unusual or creative. For example, a blue car color can be "night sky blue", or a white shirt color can be "snowy day." Why do companies choose these new color names? How does this help them sell their products?

You may need to provide additional examples of unusual color names beyond "night sky blue" and "snowy day."

Unit 4: Technology

Challenge Questions 1 and 2

1. *In this unit, you read about how technology can improve an athlete's performance. However, some people think that using technology in sports creates an unfair advantage. What are some other situations where technology could create an unfair advantage? Why?*

2. *Can technology ever hurt someone's performance? When might technology make it more difficult to do something? Explain your answer.*

Before assigning these questions, you should have students brainstorm on some ideas together. For example, in response to question 1, technology might create an unfair advantage in school when some students have access to smartphones but others do not. In response to question 2, technology might hurt someone's performance in situations such as driving a car. If a car has too many automatic features, a driver might not pay attention to the road and there could be an accident. Another example is when students rely too much on calculators and it becomes harder for them to add, subtract, multiply, and divide in their heads. You may want to provide your own examples, if needed.

Unit 5: Business

Challenge Question

Some family businesses are over 100 years old. Why do you think these companies are successful? What do these businesses do that other family businesses do not do?

Students will probably need a few examples, in addition to the ones given in the readings. You can point out, for instance, that Ford Motor Company and Walmart are family-run businesses. You can also provide examples of small family-owned restaurants, stores, and other businesses in your local area.

Unit 8: Public Health

Challenge Question

Every year, we hear about new illnesses that can spread quickly from person to person, and even around the world. What do you do when you hear about a new illness? How do you stay healthy?

Elicit from students examples of major illnesses that are contagious. Examples may include Tuberculosis, AIDS, H1N1 (Swine Flu), MERS (Middle Eastern Respiratory Syndrome), SARS (Avian Flu), or Ebola.

Posting to the Discussion Board: Student Instructions

When you post to the Discussion Board, make sure that you choose the correct unit number and the correct thread.

Logging in to the Discussion Board

1. Log in to iQ Online.

2. Choose your level.

3. Choose More (…) and then choose Discussions. Then choose Level 3 threads. (Or choose My class threads for posts by your teacher or other students.)

OR

Enter Practice and go to the Unit Question Discussion (the first activity) or the Unit Question Reflection (the last activity). Access the Discussions from the link included in these activities.

Replying to a Post

1. Choose the unit and discussion question that your teacher assigned.

2. Read the question or questions carefully. If responding to another student's post, read their response carefully.

3. Choose Add Comment.

4. Type your answer to the question or questions. Follow your teacher's instructions on how to write a good reply. If responding to another student, be sure to include their name so it is clear who you are responding to.

5. Read through your reply carefully: check the organization of your ideas, and check your spelling and grammar.

6. Choose Send.

Creating a New Discussion Topic

1. Choose New Thread.

2. In the subject line, enter the name of the thread. Be sure to choose a name that indicates clearly what the subject of the thread is (by including the unit number, for example).

3. Write your comments.

4. Choose Send.

Warning: You cannot delete your writing after you choose Send. Only the teacher can delete a thread or an individual response.

Example Discussion Board Post

Directions: Read the questions and the discussion board post. After that, answer the questions about the post.

Example Unit: Psychology

Unit Question Discussion: What are the benefits of positive thinking?

1. Describe someone you know who has a positive way of thinking. What does this person do that makes him/her a positive person?

2. How is positive thinking good for that person?

My grandfather has a positive way of thinking. He does not worry and always smiles. He is 78 years old, but he likes to learn new things. Last year, he learned how to play the guitar. He has many friends, and he likes to visit them. Every week, he has lunch with several neighbors, and every year, he travels to California to visit his best friend. He likes to tell stories about the good things in his life. He does not talk about his time in the war, but he talks about how he met his best friend there. I believe that positive thinking has helped my grandfather in many ways. I think he does not get sick because he has a positive way of thinking. I also think that he has many friends of different ages because he is a positive person. I want to be like my grandfather when I get older.

1. Has the writer answered all the questions? Underline the part that you think answers the first question, and double-underline the part that answers the second question.

2. Look at the first and last sentence of the post.

   a. What is the purpose of the first sentence? What does it tell you?

   b. What is the purpose of the last sentence? What does it tell you?

3. The writer gives examples in his/her response to the two questions.

   a. Find the examples for the first question, and number them.

   b. Find the examples for the second question and number them.

4. Overall, has the writer answered the questions completely and clearly?

   a. If yes, explain.

   b. If no, what can the writer improve?

50   Q Third Edition   **Reading and Writing 2**   Discussion Boards • Students

5. Review the rubric. Use the rubric to give a score for the post above.

> **20** = The Discussion Board writing element was completely successful (at least 90% of the time).
>
> **15** = The Discussion Board writing element was mostly successful (at least 70% of the time).
>
> **10** = The Discussion Board writing element was partially successful (at least 50% of the time).
>
> **0** = The Discussion Board writing element was not successful.

Writing a Discussion Board Post	20 points	15 points	10 points	0 points
The post answers the question(s) clearly and completely.				
The post has clear and specific explanations and examples.				
The post shows careful thinking about the topic.				
Sentences are complete and have appropriate final punctuation.				
The post correctly includes vocabulary and grammar from the unit.				
The length of the post is appropriate.				
The post includes formal and polite language.				

Total points: _____ out of _____

Follow-up:

With a partner, or in small groups, brainstorm on one of the topics below. What ideas will you include in your post?

1. Describe someone you know who has a negative way of thinking. What does this person do that makes him/her a negative person?

2. How is negative thinking bad for that person?

Teaching Notes

Unit-by-Unit teaching notes offer Expansion Activities, Multilevel Options and Background Notes to help you teach with *Q: Skills for Success Third Edition*.
Also includes Unit Assignment Rubrics.

Background Note

UNIT OPENER   pages 2–3

The photo on pp. 2–3 shows a group of journalists taking photographs and video of new iPhone models at a publicity event for Apple.

Expansion Activity 1

UNIT QUESTION   page 3

1. Introduce the Unit Question: *Why does something become popular?* Ask related information questions or questions about personal experiences to help students prepare for answering the more abstract Unit Question. For example, ask: *What was the most popular TV show last year? What's the most popular TV show right now? Why do you think it is popular?*

2. Label two pieces of poster paper *The TV show is good*; *People like what their friends like* and place them in corners of the room.

3. Ask students to read and consider the Unit Question for a moment. Say: *Let's think about this in terms of TV shows.* Have students stand in the corner next to the poster that best represents their answer to the question.

4. Direct the two groups to talk amongst themselves about the reasons for their answer. Tell them to choose a secretary to record the answers on the poster paper.

5. Call on volunteers from each group to share their opinions with the class.

6. Leave the posters up for students to refer back to at the end of the unit.

Multilevel Option 1

READING 1: Unusual Ideas to Make a Buzz
A. VOCABULARY   page 4

1. Read the directions.

2. Read each vocabulary word and have the class repeat it after you.

3. Give students time to complete the activity.

4. Go over the answers orally, asking students to read their answers.

MULTILEVEL OPTION

Group lower-level students and assist them with the task. Provide alternate example sentences to help them understand the words. *I sometimes **contribute** money to a community group. I use the phone to stay **connected** to my family. Marcus **expresses** himself through poetry. The news about the accident **spread** quickly.*

Have higher-level students complete the activity individually and then compare answers with a partner. Tell the pairs to write an additional sample sentence for each expression. Have volunteers write one of their sentences on the board. Correct the sentences with the whole class, focusing on the use of the expression rather than on other grammatical issues.

Background Note

READING 1   pages 5–6

The term *buzz* is often used in marketing to refer to the interaction of consumers and product users that increases or enhances the company's marketing message. It used to refer more to word-of-mouth consumer sharing, but these days social media is the dominant communication channel, and marketing messages that go viral can reach millions in a matter of mere days. Some of the most common tactics used to create buzz include asking bloggers to review products, creating controversy related to an industry, asking the public to choose a name or vote on something that they connect with personally, or building excitement and suspense around the launch of an event or a release date. Studies have shown a positive correlation between buzz volume and product sales or company revenue, making it an important component of any marketing message.

Multilevel Option 2

WRITE WHAT YOU THINK   page 7

1. Ask students to read the questions and reflect on their answers.

2. Model how you would like students to work in groups. Ask three students to form a group with you at the front of the class. Write on the board: *leader, note-taker, timekeeper, reporter.* Explain each job and assign jobs to the volunteers. You can be the note-taker. With this group, discuss the first question for a few minutes and write brief notes on the board. Then have the reporter summarize the answers.

3. Seat students in small groups and assign roles: a group leader to make sure everyone contributes, a note-taker to record the group's ideas, a timekeeper to watch the clock, and a reporter to share the group's ideas with the class.

4. Give students about five minutes to discuss the questions. Stop the conversations earlier if students are finishing sooner. Allow them an extra minute or two if necessary.

5. Call on each group's reporter to share ideas with the class.

6. Have each student choose one of the questions and write 5–8 sentences in response. This can be done in class or assigned as homework.

7. Call on volunteers to share their ideas with the class.

Reading Skill Note

IDENTIFYING THE MAIN IDEA OF A PARAGRAPH page 8

1. Give students a minute to read the information. Then have a volunteer read the information aloud.

2. Check comprehension by asking questions: *What is a paragraph? In Reading 1, is "advertising" a topic or a main idea? Where do you usually find the main idea of a paragraph?*

Skill Note

Identifying the main idea of a paragraph is a fundamental skill that students will practice and refine throughout the book. Identifying the main idea is the first step toward understanding the important details and main points of a reading, as well as gaining new insights about a topic. By having students identify the main idea of each paragraph as they read, they can monitor their comprehension.

Background Note

READING 2 pages 11–12

Psychologists have been studying the phenomenon of social proof since at least 1935. They have found that people tend to imitate the behavior of a group when they are unsure of how to behave. This happens regardless of whether the group's actions are the correct ones in the situation.

Expansion Activity 2

WORK WITH THE VIDEO page 15

1. Tell students that a chain is a restaurant that has locations in many different places, such as *McDonald's, KFC,* and *Starbucks.* Ask students to brainstorm restaurant or coffee shop chains that are popular around the world and list them on the board.

2. Tell students chains often change their menus and their atmosphere so that they are more popular with local residents in a particular country. For example, *Starbucks* sells the Sakura Blossom Latte in its Japan stores, but not in other countries. As another example, *McDonald's* sells chocolate mousse as a popular dessert in France.

3. Put students in small groups. Assign each group a different chain from the list on the board, or have each choose one.

4. Instruct each group to research the chain's menu and atmosphere online. Have them identify examples of how the chain changes its menu and atmosphere in different countries, including their own.

5. Have each group report their findings to the rest of the class. Finish with a follow-up discussion about what makes a restaurant chain popular in other countries. Ask: *Is it good for chains to change their menus to be more popular in other countries?*

Expansion Activity 3

WRITE WHAT YOU THINK page 16

1. Ask students to read the questions and reflect on their answers.

2. Seat students in small groups and assign roles: a group leader to make sure everyone contributes, a note-taker to record the group's ideas, a reporter to share the group's ideas with the class, and a timekeeper to watch the clock.

3. Give students about five minutes to discuss the questions. Stop the conversations earlier if students are finishing sooner. Allow them an extra minute or two if necessary.

Vocabulary Skill Note

WORD FAMILIES page 16

1. Give students a minute to read the box. Then have a volunteer read the text aloud. Explain: *A word root is the part of the word that carries the main meaning. For example, the root of "discussion" is "discuss."*

2. Check comprehension by asking questions: *Why is it important to know what part of speech a word is? Can you always tell if a word is a noun or verb by the spelling?*

Skill Note

For students, nouns and verbs are easier to learn than adverbs and adjectives. However, nouns with irregular plural forms or verbs with irregular past forms are more challenging to identify. As you work with word families, give students clues that will help them identify what part of speech they are. For example, when you introduce a countable noun, use *a/an (influence)*. When you introduce a verb, use *to (make)*. These clues will help students notice context.

Expansion Activity 4

VOCABULARY SKILL
A. IDENTIFY page 16

1. After students have completed the activity, direct them to their dictionaries or an online dictionary, such as the Oxford Learner's Dictionaries, to identify common collocations with each noun/verb pair, for example: *make a choice/choose well*, *connect with others/feel a strong connection with*, *make a contribution/contribute money to*, etc. Write a couple of examples on the board. Then have students work in pairs to identify collocations with the noun-verb pairs.

2. Ask the class to write their collocations on the board, or elicit them from the class and write them. Ask students to identify common grammatical patterns they see with nouns and verbs. For example, nouns are often preceded by articles and adjectives. Verbs are often followed by nouns (transitive verbs) and prepositional phrases (intransitive verbs).

3. Direct pairs to write sentences with 8–10 of the collocations of their choosing.

4. Ask volunteers to read their sentences aloud. Have the other students listen and identify the collocations they hear.

Writing Skill Note

WRITING A DESCRIPTIVE PARAGRAPH page 18

1. Give students a minute to read the information. Then have a volunteer read the information aloud.

2. Check comprehension: *Why do we write descriptive paragraphs? What are the elements needed in a descriptive paragraph? How do we help the reader understand the topic?*

Skill Note

As students are beginning to develop their writing skills, it is easier for them to write simple, descriptive sentences with a topic and controlling idea. Putting the topic sentence first is also the easiest placement for most students. Make sure that students always include the topic and controlling idea, and stress the importance of clarity. As students grow stronger in their writing, they can experiment with putting the topic sentence later in the paragraph.

Grammar Note

PRESENT CONTINUOUS page 21

1. Give students a minute to read the information. Have volunteers read the information aloud.

2. Check comprehension: *What do we use for activities in progress? How do we form the present continuous?*

Skill Note

Explain to students that some verbs are commonly used in the simple present to express states and conditions: *have, know, understand, like, love, see, taste, hear, smell, own*. These verbs do not express action; they are not used in the present continuous.

Multilevel Option 3

WRITE page 24

1. Go over the directions with the class. You may want to have students write on every other line (or use double spacing on a computer) so that it is easier to make corrections and revisions. Students can write during class or at home.

2. Have students read their writing aloud in small groups. Encourage students to ask questions about each other's writing.

3. Give students time to make any improvements on their writing.

MULTILEVEL OPTION

Group lower-level students together so that you can assist them as they write. While they are working on the topic sentence, circulate and help them as needed. Check each student's topic sentence. Then assist students as needed while they write their paragraphs. Have higher-level students write two paragraphs about two different trends. When students have finished, ask for volunteers from both groups to share their writing.

Unit Assignment Rubrics

Unit 1   Marketing

Unit Assignment Rubric

Student name: _____

Date: _____

Unit Assignment: *Write a paragraph describing a current trend and why it is popular.*

20 points = Writing was completely successful (at least 90% of the time).
15 points = Writing was mostly successful (at least 70% of the time).
10 points = Writing was partially successful (at least 50% of the time).
  0 points = Writing was not successful.

Write a Descriptive Paragraph	20 points	15 points	10 points	0 points
The topic sentence has a clear topic and controlling idea.				
There is a clear description of the trend and why it is popular.				
The first line of the paragraph is indented.				
Each sentence has correct capitalization and punctuation.				
Words are correctly spelled.				

Total points: _____

Comments:

Background Note

UNIT OPENER pages 26–27

The photo on pp. 26–27 shows a portrait of a mature woman dancing, smiling, and having fun. She is wearing a long-sleeved yellow sweater, black pants, and a pair of black eyeglasses.

Expansion Activity 1

UNIT QUESTION page 27

1. Introduce the Unit Question: *How do colors affect our behavior?* Ask related information questions or questions about personal experiences to help students prepare for answering the more abstract Unit Question. For example, ask: *What color clothing do you wear to school? To work? To a fancy dinner? On a daily basis? Why do people choose different colors for different situations? Do colors make you act differently in different situations? Does a particular color make you act more confident, more reserved, or shyer?*

2. On the board, write different colors on the board, such as *red*, *black*, *white*, and *yellow*. As students describe different situations, write them on the board under the appropriate color.

3. Ask students questions about the colors and their effects on their behavior. For example, *does red make you act more confidently? Does black make you feel more sophisticated? Do you expect people in black to act in a more sophisticated way?*

4. Post the lists to refer back to later in the unit.

Expansion Activity 2

A. page 27

1. Read the first two questions. Call on a few students to give their answers and then have a student ask you the questions. Model answering the questions.

2. Put students in pairs or small groups to discuss the first two questions.

3. Call on volunteers to share their ideas with the class. Ask additional questions: *What is your least favorite color? Why don't you like the color?*

4. Focus students' attention on the photo. Have a volunteer describe the photo to the class. Read the question aloud. Have volunteers give their answers.

Multilevel Option 1

READING 1: What Colors Do You Like to Wear?
A. VOCABULARY page 28

1. Ask a student to read the directions. Then give students time to do the activity. Remind them not to use their dictionaries during the activity.

2. Go over the answers with the class.

3. Have students identify each vocabulary word as a noun, verb, or adjective.

MULTILEVEL OPTION

Group lower-level students and assist them with the task. Provide alternate example sentences to help them understand the words. *When I lived in Japan, I learned about Japanese **culture**. Coffee **affects** me; when I drink it, I can't sleep at night. I like to wear a variety of colors, including red, green, and white. When I read a good book, I am **unaware** of the time.*

Have higher-level students complete the activity individually and then compare answers with a partner. Have pairs write an additional sample sentence for each word. Have volunteers write one of their sentences on the board. Correct the sentences with the whole class, focusing on the use of the expression rather than on other grammatical issues.

Background Note

READING 1 pages 30–31

Although there are many theories and ideas about how colors affect us, the scientific research to support them is scarce. Studies in color psychology have shown that results are also determined by culture, and people from different cultures will attribute different meanings to the same color. For example, depending on the culture, the color blue might represent trust and security, sadness and depression, or good health and immortality. Likewise, the color red can mean passion and energy in Western cultures, but in Asian cultures, red tends to represent luck, celebration, and longevity.

Another example is purple. Many countries, such as Japan, associate purple with wealth and nobility, while in other countries, such as Brazil and Thailand, purple is the color of mourning (death).

Multilevel Option 2

 WRITE WHAT YOU THINK page 33

1. Ask students to read the questions and reflect on their answers.

2. If you think it would be helpful for your students, model how you would like them to work in groups. Ask three students to form a group with you at the front of the class. Write on the board: *leader, note-taker, timekeeper, reporter.* Explain each job and assign jobs to the volunteers. You can be the note-taker. With this group, discuss the first question for four minutes and write brief notes on the board. Then have the reporter summarize the answers.

3. Seat students in small groups and assign roles: a group leader to make sure everyone contributes, a note-taker to record the group's ideas, a timekeeper to watch the clock, and a reporter to share the group's ideas with the class.

4. Give students about five minutes to discuss the questions. Stop the conversations earlier if students are finishing sooner. Allow them an extra minute or two if necessary.

5. Call on each group's reporter to share ideas with the class.

6. Have each student choose one of the questions and write 5–8 sentences in response. This can be done in class or assigned as homework.

7. Call on volunteers to share ideas with the class.

MULTILEVEL OPTION

For step 5, work together with lower-level students to answer question 2. As you discuss different colors, write notes on the board. Then have the group form sentences for the answer.

For higher-level students, have students write individual answers. Then have them compare and discuss their answers. Encourage them to expand and improve their answers, rewriting them before handing them in.

Reading Skill Note

GETTING MEANING FROM CONTEXT   page 33

1. Give students a minute to read the information.

2. Check comprehension by asking questions: *What is context? Can context give you the exact meaning of a word? Why should you use context to try to understand the meaning of unfamiliar words instead of using a dictionary? How can using context improve your reading?*

Skill Note

Getting meaning from context is a strategy that students should learn to use when they encounter an unfamiliar word. However, the context does not always

provide a usable clue. Sometimes, there is no clue at all, and students may need to do what fluent readers do: ignore the word and keep on reading. For students, the most helpful clues are those that are found in the same sentence. They can be synonyms, restatements, examples, or explanations.

Background Note

READING 2   page 36

Colors are a very important aspect of a company brand. Businesses spend a great deal of time and money to develop a distinct brand. Branding includes colors, the company name, the text style of the name, a logo design, and sometimes a motto.

Multilevel Option 3

B. IDENTIFY   page 37

1. Remind students that the main idea of a reading is the writer's comment on the topic.

2. Ask students to read and complete the activity individually.

3. Go over the answer with the class.

MULTILEVEL OPTION

Group lower-level students together and assist them with the task. Discuss each choice and talk about why it is or is not the main idea.

For higher-level students, have them close their books and work in pairs to write their own sentences stating the main idea. Have several students write their sentences on the board and discuss their answers as a class. Then they can check their answers by looking at the activity in the book.

Expansion Activity 3

WORK WITH THE VIDEO   page 39

1. Put students into small groups. Have each group to decide on what the color of the (current) year should be.

2. Bring various magazines into class, or have groups visit magazines online. Have them look for color trends in advertisements, such as those for fashion, makeup, and home furnishings. They may also look for color trends in products, product packaging, and graphic design.

3. Have each group choose their color of the year. Ask them to give the color a specific name and write a 2–3 sentence description of the color. Encourage them to explain why the color represents a specific aspect of the world today. For example, Pantone's 2019 color of the year was "Living Coral," a bright color that reflected the intricate communities of coral reef ecosystems, a statement on people's need to have and maintain lively connections in today's social media age.

4. Ask each group to create a poster with images from magazines or other sources that illustrate their color of the year. Have them put the name of the color at

the top of their poster, as well as specific adjectives that describe the color and its connection to today's society.

5. Have students put their posters up around the room and ask the class to go around and vote on the color they think should be color of the year. Ask for one representative of each poster to stand by the poster to explain their color to others.

6. Take a final vote and announce the color of the year, according to the team with the most votes.

Vocabulary Skill Note

SUFFIXES page 40

1. Give students time to silently read the vocabulary information. Then have volunteers read the text aloud. Explain: *Learning common suffixes is a good way to increase your vocabulary. It can also help you guess the meaning of a word in a sentence.*

2. Check comprehension by asking questions: *What are the suffixes in this box? Is a suffix always at the end of a word? What happens to a word when you add a suffix?*

Skill Note

Suffixes that change a word's part of speech are challenging for students because there are many different suffixes used in English. For example, the suffixes *-al, -ful, -y, -less, -ward,* and *-ern* can all be used to make adjectives. Which suffix should be used is not always predictable, making it confusing for students. It's best to focus on the most commonly used suffixes and to help students become aware of different word parts.

Writing Skill Note

BRAINSTORMING page 42

1. Give students time to read the information. Then have a volunteer read the text aloud.

2. Check comprehension: *How would you use listing? What goes in the center circle of an idea map? When can we use freewriting?*

Skill Note

Brainstorming through freewriting is a very useful way to generate ideas about a topic. It's helpful to focus on a specific question or topic during freewriting. For some students, freewriting may be more difficult to do than speaking. Encourage students to just focus on ideas and not to worry about spelling or grammar. Some students may want to use their native language for certain terms or expressions. Later they can consult a dictionary.

Grammar Note

FUTURE WITH *WILL* page 44

1. Have volunteers read the information. You can ask higher-level students to give additional example sentences.

2. Check comprehension by asking questions: *What form of verb follows* will *to make a promise? What is the contraction for* will?

Skill Note

Point out that we use *will* to talk about future plans, to make predictions, to make promises, and to make offers or volunteer to do something (e.g., *We need a catcher for next week's game. I'll get Jason to come.*). In some cases, we can replace *will* with *[be] going to* for specific plans in the near future (e.g., *I will have dinner with Carmen* or *I am going to have dinner with Carmen.*).

Unit Assignment Rubrics

Unit 2   Psychology

Unit Assignment Rubric

Student name: _____

Date: _____

Unit Assignment: *Create a business and write a proposal explaining the colors you will use and why.*

20 points = Writing was completely successful (at least 90% of the time).
15 points = Writing was mostly successful (at least 70% of the time).
10 points = Writing was partially successful (at least 50% of the time).
 0 points = Writing was not successful.

Write a Proposal for a Business	20 points	15 points	10 points	0 points
The description of the business is easy to understand.				
There is a clear explanation of the business colors and why they were chosen.				
Each sentence has correct capitalization and punctuation.				
Words are correctly spelled.				
The future with *will* is used correctly.				

Total points: _____

Comments:

Background Note

UNIT OPENER pages 50–51

The photo on pp. 50–51 shows a woman throwing a plastic water bottle out of her car window. The background shows a desolate, desert-like environment.

Expansion Activity 1

UNIT QUESTION page 51

1. Introduce the Unit Question: *What does it mean to be polite?* Ask related information questions or questions about personal experiences to help students prepare for answering the more abstract Unit Question. For example, ask: *What are some examples of polite behavior? Do you know someone who is very polite? What does the person do to be polite?*

2. To help students formulate answers, write on the board: *Being polite means _____ing…/Being polite means not _____ing…*

3. Put students in small groups and give each group a piece of poster paper and a marker.

4. Give students a minute to silently consider their answers to the Unit Question. Tell students to pass the paper and the marker around the group. Direct each group member to write a different answer to the question. Encourage them to help one another.

5. Ask each group to choose a reporter to read the answers to the class. Point out similarities and differences among the answers. If answers from different groups are similar, make a group list that incorporates all of the answers. Post the list to refer to later in the unit.

Expansion Activity 2

A. page 51

1. Read the two questions. Call on a few students to give their answers.

2. Put students in pairs or small groups to discuss the first two questions.

3. Call on volunteers to share their ideas with the class. Ask additional questions: *What would be the polite thing to do? How did this person teach you politeness? Was it by example, or was it by telling you what to do?*

4. Focus students' attention on the photo. Have a volunteer describe the photo to the class. Read the questions aloud and have students answer them. Ask: *Is it OK to throw trash from your car? How do you feel when you see people do it? Do you think it is rude? Why or why not?*

21ST CENTURY SKILLS EXPANSION

Communication skills are highly valued in the workplace and are key skills for the 21st century. Eighty percent of business executives said that communication skills are important in measuring an employee's performance. Knowing how to be polite is an important component of good communication. In addition, understanding cultural differences in manners and etiquette is especially valuable in today's global economy. In this unit, students will explore the question of what it means to be polite.

Multilevel Option 1

READING 1: Being Polite from Culture to Culture
A. VOCABULARY page 52

1. Ask a student to read the directions. Then give students time to do the activity. Remind them not to use their dictionaries during the activity.

2. Go over the answers with the class.

MULTILEVEL OPTION

Group lower-level students and assist them with the task. Provide alternate example sentences to help them understand the words. *I feel **awkward** when I am with people I don't know. My grandfather made sure that we used good table **manners**. The police officer noticed the man's strange **behavior** in the bank. I hope I **make a good impression** when I have a job interview.*

Have higher-level students complete the activity individually and then compare answers with a partner. Have pairs write an additional sample sentence for each word. Have volunteers write their sentences on the board for review.

Background Note

READING 1 pages 53–54

The book mentioned in this reading, *Kiss, Bow, or Shake Hands: The Bestselling Guide to Doing Business in More Than 60 Countries* (1994 edition) by Terri Morrison, Wayne A. Conaway, and George A. Borden, is a popular guide to different cultures and customs. It is used by business people, governments, business schools, and travelers. Its popularity reflects the interest in and necessity for intercultural understanding in today's global economy.

Background Note

READING 2 pages 60–61

There is a wealth of information for travelers online, including a wide variety of websites dedicated to providing travel information and tips. Most of these websites have online discussion groups where users can post questions. Questions are then answered by other users. Some popular travel websites are Trip Advisor, Travelzine, Lonely Planet, Fodor's, Rough Guides, and Let's Go.

Multilevel Option 2

B. CATEGORIZE page 61

1. Ask students to read and complete the activity individually.

2. Go over the answers with the class.

MULTILEVEL OPTION

Group lower-level students together and assist them with the task. Discuss each choice and talk about whether it's true or false.

For higher-level students, have them do the activity without looking back at the reading. Have them correct the false statements to make them true. When they have finished, have students compare them and then check them against the reading.

Expansion Activity 3

WORK WITH THE VIDEO page 63

1. Tell students they are going to make a list of rules for the use of cell phones in their classroom. Remind students that rules are often written in the imperative form, e.g., *Put your phone on silent when you enter the class, Do not take calls during class, Put your phone away during lectures,* etc.

2. Have students work in groups of three to discuss proper "phone etiquette" in the classroom. Have each group brainstorm a list of 4–6 rules. Assign roles to the students: a moderator to encourage everyone's participation, a note-taker to take notes on the ideas they share, and a reporter to report their ideas to the rest of the class. Circulate and help groups as necessary, such as with vocabulary or specific wording they might need to express their ideas.

3. Give each group a piece of poster paper and a marker, preferably a different color each. Have each group list their rules on their poster paper in large, legible writing. Tell them to give their poster a title, such as *Cell Phone Rules, Classroom Phone Rules, Phone Etiquette,* etc. Tell them that one of the posters will be the winner and will stay up in the classroom for the rest of the term!

4. Have each group put their posters up on the wall and/or board. Then ask each reporter to present their list of rules to the class, explaining why each rule is important. Get them to identify what behavior the rule is trying to prevent.

5. Finally, have the class vote on which group's rules they like the best. Keep the winning poster up on the wall and refer to it as necessary in future classes if students aren't following the rules they agreed upon.

Vocabulary Skill Note

PREFIXES page 64

1. Give students time to read the information. Then have volunteers read the text aloud. Explain: *Learning common prefixes is a good way to increase your vocabulary. It can also help you guess the meaning of a word in a sentence.*

2. Check comprehension by asking questions: *What are the three prefixes here? When do you use the prefix im-?*

Skill Note

Prefixes can help students expand their vocabulary, but they can also be confusing and unpredictable. For example, *mis-, dis-,* and *un-* are all negative, but they have slightly different meanings and are not interchangeable (*misunderstand, dislike, unable*). The prefixes taught here (*in-, im-, un-*) all carry the meaning "not."

Expansion Activity 4

B. APPLY page 65

1. Read the directions. Give students time to do the activity without consulting their dictionaries.

2. Go over the answers with the class.

WORD BUILDING

1. Choose five to ten additional words with prefixes to teach your students. Select words that have a stem that will be familiar to students. Choose words appropriate to the level of your students. Here is a list of possible words: *improper, impatient, incomplete, inconsiderate, inconvenient, incorrect, insensitive, unsure, unsafe, untrue, unimportant, unhealthy, unaware, uncertain, unhappy.*

2. Write the words on the board and elicit the meanings from students. Then have students check a dictionary for the definition.

3. Have each student choose three words to include in sentences.

4. Ask volunteers to share their sentences.

Writing Skill Note

SUPPORTING YOUR MAIN IDEA WITH EXAMPLES page 66

1. Give students time to silently read the information. Then have a volunteer read the example aloud.

2. Check comprehension: *Why do we use examples when we write? What are two ways to introduce an example?*

Skill Note

Supporting an idea with examples is a very common paragraph technique. It is useful in many types of writing, from history to science. Examples should be clearly linked to the main idea of the paragraph, and examples should be adequately explained. *For example* and *for instance* are the most commonly used expressions for introducing examples in academic writing.

Grammar Note

SUBJECT-VERB AGREEMENT page 69

1. Have volunteers read the information.
2. Check comprehension: *Is the subject always before the verb? Does a plural noun always end with -s? What is the plural form of* woman?

Skill Note

There is/are sentences are tricky for learners because the subject comes after the verb. When editing their writing, students need to check such sentences carefully by first identifying the subject. With *there is/ are*, the verb agrees with the subject that is the closest. *There **is** a **bank*** and two stores. *There **are** two **stores** and a bank.*

Unit Assignment Rubrics

Unit 3   Social Psychology

Unit Assignment Rubric

Student name: _____

Date: _____

Unit Assignment: *Write a paragraph in response to a question on an online discussion board about politeness.*

20 points = Writing was completely successful (at least 90% of the time).
15 points = Writing was mostly successful (at least 70% of the time).
10 points = Writing was partially successful (at least 50% of the time).
 0 points = Writing was not successful.

Write a Paragraph with Supporting Examples	20 points	15 points	10 points	0 points
There is a clear topic sentence that answers the question about politeness.				
There are at least two examples to support the main idea.				
Each sentence has correct capitalization and punctuation.				
Words are correctly spelled.				
Each sentence has subject-verb agreement.				

Total points: _____

Comments:

Background Note

UNIT OPENER pages 74–75

The photo on pp. 74–75 shows a young Russian female athlete trying on a virtual reality (VR) headset at the Olympic Park's media center in Sochi, Russia ahead of the 2017 World Festival for Youth and Students.

Expansion Activity 1

UNIT QUESTION page 75

1. Introduce the Unit Question: *How can technology improve performance?* Say: *Let's start off our discussion by listing different kinds of technology that help students learn a new language.*

2. Seat students in small groups and direct them to pass around a paper as quickly as they can, with each group member adding one item to the list. Tell them they have two minutes to make the lists and that they should write as many ideas as possible.

3. Call time and ask a reporter from each group to read the list aloud.

4. Use ideas from the lists as a springboard for discussion. Have students identify the advantages and disadvantages of each kind of technology. For example, ask: *Which type of technology helps you the most to learn English? Which ones are less helpful? Why?*

5. Make a master list of the items from the lists. Post the list to refer back to later in the unit.

Multilevel Option 1

READING 1: Virtual Reality for Medical Students
A. VOCABULARY page 76

1. Ask a student to read the directions. Then give students time to do the activity.

2. Go over the answers with the class.

MULTILEVEL OPTION

Group lower-level students and assist them with the task. Provide alternate example sentences to help them understand the words. *The students' **performance** on the test was low, so the teacher reviewed the material again. Many schools have **replaced** traditional books with e-books that students can get for free. When you write, it is important to give **specific** details so others can understand your ideas clearly. The doctors were **under pressure** not to make any mistakes when they performed heart surgery on the patient.*

Have higher-level students complete the activity individually and then compare their answers with a partner. Have pairs write an additional sample sentence for each word. Have volunteers write sentences on the board for review.

Background Note

READING 1 pages 77–78

Even though virtual reality devices have been around since the 1960s, the term "virtual reality" was not coined until 1982, when it appeared in the science fiction novel, *The Judas Mandala*, by Damien Broderick. Between 1970 and 1990, VR devices were used largely for medical simulation for doctors, flight simulation for airline and NASA pilots, and for military training purposes. Over the last 25 years, virtual reality technology has advanced rapidly, particularly with the development of "augmented reality," a type of VR that blends the computer-generated digital environment with a user's physical surroundings, creating an even more realistic experience.

Some of the biggest advancements in VR have come from the gaming industry. Most VR gaming consoles consist of a large headset with a small screen in front of the eyes, which allows users to interact in three-dimensional environments. One of the most advanced VR consoles is the Oculus Rift, a VR headset which includes integrated headphones and handheld accessories with sensors that simulate the players' body movements in the virtual environment. Other popular VR gaming consoles are manufactured by PlayStation, Sega, and Nintendo. In addition to gaming, some VR consoles can be used to watch movies, many of which can be viewed in 360 degrees. Another modern application of VR is virtual reality therapy, a psychological treatment for those who suffer from anxiety, depression, and post-traumatic stress disorder. Psychologists can use controlled VR environments both to diagnose mental disorders and to create tasks that can help treat conditions through exposure to particular stressors.

Multilevel Option 2

WRITE WHAT YOU THINK page 80

1. Ask students to read the questions and reflect on their answers.

2. Seat students in small groups and assign roles: a group leader to make sure everyone contributes, a note-taker to record the group's ideas, a timekeeper to watch the clock, and a reporter to share the group's ideas with the class.

3. Give students about five minutes to discuss the questions. Stop the conversations earlier if students are finishing sooner. Allow them an extra minute or two if necessary.

4. Call on each group's reporter to share ideas with the class.

5. Have each student choose one of the questions and write 5–8 sentences in response. This can be done in class or assigned as homework.

6. Call on volunteers to share answers with the class.

Work together with lower-level students to answer the questions. Elicit ideas from students and write them on the board. Then have students decide which ideas to include in each of the two answers. Circle these ideas. With help from the students, write out the answers on the board and have students copy them.

Have higher-level students work in pairs to answer both questions. Remind them to give specific examples in their answers. When students have finished, ask for volunteers from both groups to share their answers. After that, students can expand and improve their answers, revising them before handing them in.

Reading Skill Note

TAKING NOTES page 81

1. Ask a student to read the information aloud.

2. Check comprehension by asking questions: *Where can you write your notes? What are some things to note while you read? Why is it a good idea to take notes?*

3. Ask students about their own experience with taking notes. Ask questions such as: *In what classes do you need to take notes? Do you usually write in your book or in a notebook? Some people are very good at taking notes. Are any of you good at taking notes? What tips can you give your classmates?*

Skill Note

Note-taking is a valuable skill for any student who reads in order to learn new material. It is a way to monitor comprehension and review important points after reading. Note-taking can also give students a quick visual outline of the important points. The difficulty for many students is knowing what to take notes on. For this reason, direct instruction and practice in note-taking is helpful.

Expansion Activity 2

THE TECHNOLOGY ADVANTAGE
A. VOCABULARY   page 82

1. Ask a student to read the directions aloud.

2. Give students time to do the activity. Remind students not to use their dictionaries during the activity.

3. Go over the answers with the class.

VOCABULARY NOTEBOOKS

1. Have students start (or add to) a vocabulary notebook. Explain: *A vocabulary notebook will help you remember and use new words. You need to use a new word many times before you can remember it.*

2. Draw a table on the board with these headings at the top of columns: *Word and part of speech; Definition; Example sentence; Other word forms.* Have volunteers come to the board to fill in information for one of the vocabulary words.

3. Give students time to write in a vocabulary notebook. They can finish adding new words at home.

4. From time to time, check their notebooks to follow their progress.

Background Note

READING 2   pages 84–85

The unfair advantage an athlete or team may gain from the use of technology is referred to these days as "technology doping." Since most sports require some sort of equipment, and better, safer equipment can be considered a good thing for a sport, what actually constitutes technology doping is quite often a judgment call. Currently, the decision to allow or ban a new technology and to set standardized materials and dimensions falls to each sport's own governing body. This will definitely be a topic to monitor in the years to come.

Multilevel Option 3

B. IDENTIFY   page 85

1. Ask students to complete the activity individually.

2. Have volunteers come to the board and write their answers.

Group lower-level students together into pairs to complete the task and assist as necessary. For higher-level students, have them work individually. Then have them identify which notes express main ideas, and which ones give supporting details. Have students write a sentence that states the main idea of the whole text, using the main ideas they identified in the activity to help them.

Expansion Activity 3

WORK WITH THE VIDEO   page 87

1. Tell students they are going to brainstorm real and imaginary uses of GPS in different situations. Topics could include *mobile gaming, farming, sales, tourism, education, public safety, medicine,* etc.

2. Put 4–5 poster papers on the wall and write the name of a different topic on each one, or dictate them to students to write them for you.

3. Put the students into small groups. Tell them they will spend five minutes at each station. Each group will brainstorm possible uses of GPS in each situation and write their ideas on the poster paper. Encourage them to write key words and phrases to express their ideas rather than complete sentences.

4. Use a timer and call time when students should rotate to the next station. Rotate until each group has added their ideas at each station. Circulate and help as necessary.

5. Bring the whole class back together. Ask students which uses are the most useful, the most difficult, the most unlikely, etc.

6. Have students choose one of the situations and write a short paragraph. Have them answer the Unit Question—*How can technology improve performance?* —in relation to the use of GPS they chose. Collect the paragraphs and provide feedback on the students' ideas and their ability to apply a specific application of GPS to the Unit Question.

Vocabulary Skill Note

USING THE DICTIONARY page 88

1. Give students time to read the information. Then have a volunteer read the text aloud.

2. Ask: *Which nouns are used with* financial *in the example sentences?* (difficulties, aid, apply) *Have you heard these expressions before? Example sentences in dictionaries will show the most common word combinations.*

3. Ask students what additional information they find the most useful. Students will most likely have different opinions.

Skill Note

Although most students know the basics of using a dictionary, it is a worthwhile use of class time to model and practice dictionary skills. For example, in addition to knowing the abbreviations and using the notes in a definition, students can gain a deeper understanding of a word by reading the example sentences. They also should be reminded to look at the context in which a word is used in order to choose the correct definition.

Expansion Activity 4

A. APPLY page 89

1. Read the directions and give students five minutes to do the activity.

2. Go over the answers for items 1–3 with the class.

3. Have volunteers go to the board to write their sentences. Discuss the word usage and help students correct any errors.

21ST CENTURY SKILLS EXPANSION

Communication skills are highly valued in the workplace. If good oral skills are not mirrored in good written skills, an employee will have a difficult time advancing in a career. Employees need to communicate clearly in writing, from emails to reports. Students with good dictionary skills will have a useful resource for improving their communication skills. By modeling and emphasizing dictionary use, you will help students become independent learners.

Writing Skill Note

WRITING AN OPINION PARAGRAPH page 90

1. Have volunteers read the information and examples aloud.

2. Check comprehension: *How do you support your opinion when you write? Why do you think it's a good idea to restate your opinion at the end of your paragraph?*

Skill Note

Writing an opinion paragraph is a common assignment in an academic setting. However, how a student goes about presenting and supporting an opinion may differ from culture to culture. In North America and in the Western world, students are expected to present their opinions very directly and offer strong support. In other cultures, writers may approach the task differently, starting with an exploration of several different opinions before presenting their own. It is important for writers to understand what their audience expects, as this will affect how their opinion paragraph should be organized.

Grammar Note

MODALS page 93

1. Have a volunteer read the information aloud.

2. Check comprehension: *Which modal is more common:* should *or* ought to? *Which modal do we use for strong statements?*

Skill Note

Modals are helping verbs that are used with verbs to change the meaning of the principal verb. Unlike regular verbs, modals are not conjugated. Also, they are followed by another verb without *to*. Students often have trouble with modals since modals may overlap in meaning and have subtle differences. In addition, the same modal may have more than one meaning. For example, *must* can be used to express an obligation or a conclusion. Making a strong opinion statement with *must* is more common in writing than in conversation. *Ought to* is not as common in academic writing.

Unit Assignment Rubrics

Unit 4   Technology

Unit Assignment Rubric

Student name: _____

Date: _____

Unit Assignment: *Write an opinion paragraph about how technology can improve performance.*

20 points = Writing was completely successful (at least 90% of the time).
15 points = Writing was mostly successful (at least 70% of the time).
10 points = Writing was partially successful (at least 50% of the time).
 0 points = Writing was not successful.

Write an Opinion Paragraph	20 points	15 points	10 points	0 points
The topic sentence clearly states the writer's opinion about how technology can improve performance.				
There are at least two reasons to support the opinion.				
Reasons are supported with specific details and examples.				
Modals are used correctly and effectively.				
Each sentence has subject-verb agreement.				

Total points: _____

Comments:

Background Note

UNIT OPENER pages 98–99

The photo on pp. 98–99 shows a father and his son working in the kitchen of their family-owned bakery. There are several piles of bread dough on a large butcher-block table. The son is using his hands to mold some of the dough. The father is holding a dough cutter in his hand. To the left is a scale to measure the dough.

Expansion Activity 1

UNIT QUESTION page 99

1. Put students in small groups and give each group a piece of poster paper and a marker.

2. Read the Unit Question aloud: *What makes a family business successful?* Give students a minute to silently consider their answers to the Unit Question. Tell students to pass the paper and the marker around the group. Direct each group member to write a different answer to the question. Encourage students to help one another.

3. Ask each group to choose a reporter to read the answers to the class. Point out similarities and differences among the answers. If answers from different groups are similar, make a group list that incorporates all of the answers. Post the list to refer back to later in the unit.

Expansion Activity 2

A. VOCABULARY page 100

1. Explain: *When you learn a new word, notice the context it is in. You might see that some words are frequently found together. This group of words is called a* collocation. *Add information about collocations to your vocabulary notebook to help you remember words and expand your vocabulary.*

2. Ask questions about each word in the vocabulary activity and write notes on the board. For example, ask: *1. When else do we show courage?* (in sports, in difficult situations) *2. What else can you design?* (a magazine, a garden, a company brand, a store) *3. What other kinds of things can a person be an expert on?* (medicine, computers, business) *4. Where else do we see unity?* (in a sports team, in a country, in a club) *5. What other things can expand?* (a road, a room, an idea, a paragraph, vocabulary) *6. What are some examples of personal strengths?* (positive attitude, courage, being responsible) *7. What's the difference between a corporation and a business?* (A corporation is a legal arrangement. A corporation is owned by a large group of people. A business is privately owned by any number of people.) *8. What else do you sometimes manage?* (money, time, employees)

3. Give students time to make notes in their notebooks about words and collocations.

Multilevel Option 1

READING 1: A Successful Family Business
A. VOCABULARY page 100

1. Ask a student to read the directions. Then give students time to do the activity. Remind them not to use their dictionaries during the activity.

2. Go over the answers with the class.

> **MULTILEVEL OPTION**
>
> Group lower-level students and assist them with the task. Provide alternate example sentences to help them understand the words. *I like to **design** my own clothing. The business is going to **expand** and move to a bigger building. In my family, my father **manages** the finances and the checkbook. My mother's **strength** is her ability to organize large family dinners.*
>
> Have higher-level students complete the activity individually and then compare answers with a partner. Have pairs write an additional example sentence for each word. Have volunteers write one of their sentences on the board. Correct the sentences with the whole class, focusing on the use of the expression rather than on other grammatical issues.

Background Note

READING 1 pages 102–103

Small businesses can be a great way for families to work toward financial success. In fact, some of the world's largest corporations began as small family businesses. Some examples are the Korean information technology company Samsung Electronics, the French fashion and cosmetics company Dior, and the Indian energy company Reliance Industries.

Multilevel Option 2

 WRITE WHAT YOU THINK page 105

1. Ask students to read the questions and reflect on their answers.

2. Seat students in small groups and assign roles: a group leader to make sure everyone contributes, a note-taker to record the group's ideas, a timekeeper to watch the clock, and a reporter to share the group's ideas with the class.

3. Give students about five minutes to discuss the questions. Stop the conversations earlier if students are finishing sooner. Allow them an extra minute or two if necessary.

4. Call on each group's reporter to share ideas with the class.

5. Have each student choose one of the questions and write 5–8 sentences in response. This can be done in class or assigned as homework.

6. Call on volunteers to share ideas with the class.

Background Note

READING 2 pages 107–108

The Wall Street Journal is a daily newspaper that has been published since 1889. It was founded by Charles Dow, Edward Jones, and Charles Bergstresser. It was owned by the Bancroft family for over a century. It features news about the United States and international finance and business. It has the largest circulation of any newspaper in the U.S. It is named after Wall Street in New York City, which is the heart of the city's financial district. Its main competitor is the London-based *Financial Times*.

Multilevel Option 3

C. IDENTIFY page 109

1. Read the directions. Say: *Look back at the reading for your answers. Be sure your answers come from the reading, not from your own ideas.*

2. Give students two minutes to complete the activity.

3. Have volunteers draw their pie charts on the board. Discuss the answers.

Expansion Activity 3

WORK WITH THE VIDEO page 110

1. Tell students they will work in pairs to role-play an interview between the CEO of Lindt and a business reporter writing an article about the company's story and history.

2. Have students take out a piece of paper and write down the question words: *Who? What? When? Where? Why? How?* Tell students to leave plenty of space between each question.

3. Play the video again. Instruct students to take notes about the story of Lindt and tell them to put each note next to the correct question word. For example, next to *"Where"* students might write *Zurich, Switzerland,* and *Kilchberg.* Next to *"Who?"* students might write *Rudolf Spruengli* or *Johann.* If necessary, play the video a second time.

4. Have students compare their notes in pairs. Then instruct students to create interview questions using their notes, *e.g., Who started the Lindt company? What does Lindt make? What do master chocolate makers do? When did Lindt start? Where does Lindt sell its products? Where does Lindt have factories? Why is Lindt successful? How did the company grow? How much money does Lindt make?* Circulate and help students as necessary.

5. Elicit the students' questions and write them on the board, or ask for two volunteer students to write them down. Correct or amend questions as necessary.

6. Finally, have students work in pairs. One student will be the Lindt CEO and the other the reporter/interviewer. Have the reporter ask 5–6 questions from the board. Allow lower-level students to refer to their notes as they answer the questions as the CEO. Then have students switch roles. If pairs finish early, have them interview again using a different set of questions from the board.

Vocabulary Skill Note

USING THE DICTIONARY page 113

1. Give students time to read the information. Then have volunteers read the text aloud. Explain: *There is a lot of useful information in the dictionary. When you look up a word, pay attention to the grammatical information as well as the definitions.*

2. Check comprehension by asking questions: *What do C and U stand for? What kinds of irregular forms are in the dictionary?*

Skill Note

Dictionary skills are important to teach so that students become familiar with the wealth of information available. Learner's dictionaries usually have a guide to abbreviations on the inside of the front or back cover. Usually, the front of the dictionary has a guide to the various types of grammatical information, with clear examples. The appendices often have lists of irregular verbs, prefixes and suffixes, punctuation, maps, pronunciation keys, and so on.

Grammar Note

COMPARATIVE AND SUPERLATIVE ADJECTIVES page 117

1. Give students time to read the information. Then have volunteers read the text aloud.

2. Check comprehension by asking questions: *When do we use comparative adjectives? When do we use superlative adjectives? What article do we always use with superlative adjectives?*

Skill Note

Note that students often incorrectly add *more* before short comparative adjectives. For example, they may say things like *more bigger* and *more better*. Explain to students that saying *more* and *-er* together is like repeating yourself—you don't need to say it twice. Remind students that we use *more* with long (2+ syllable) adjectives only, not short (1- syllable) adjectives. Point out that we can use *much* before both forms to show a larger difference, e.g., *much bigger* and *much more expensive*.

Unit Assignment Rubrics

Unit 5   Business

Unit Assignment Rubric

Student name: _____

Date: _____

Unit Assignment: *Write a plan for a new family business.*

20 points = Writing was completely successful (at least 90% of the time).
15 points = Writing was mostly successful (at least 70% of the time).
10 points = Writing was partially successful (at least 50% of the time).
 0 points = Writing was not successful.

Write a Plan for a Family Business	20 points	15 points	10 points	0 points
There is a clear explanation of the family business and why it will be successful.				
Transition words are used to unify the plan and help the ideas flow smoothly.				
Each sentence has correct capitalization and punctuation.				
Words are correctly spelled.				
Comparative and superlative adjectives are formed correctly.				

Total points: _____

Comments:

Background Note

UNIT OPENER pages 122–123

The photo on pp. 122–123 shows a group of students reading and discussing a book in a school library. Several students are holding their books open to the same page to discuss the topics and themes discussed in the book. There is a tablet computer with headphones sitting on the table.

Expansion Activity 1

UNIT QUESTION page 123

1. Read the Unit Question aloud: *How can you learn faster and better?* Give students a minute to silently consider their answers to the Unit Question. Say: *Think about your own learning. What helps you to learn something faster? For example, what things do you do to learn new vocabulary faster?*

2. Have students work in pairs to share their answers and make a list of the things they do to learn new words more quickly.

3. Elicit student answers. Write the title "Vocabulary Learning Strategies" on the board, and write the students' ideas below it. Examples might include: *read often, use the word in speaking or writing, keep a vocabulary journal, learn roots and suffixes, use a thesaurus, visualize words,* etc.

4. Have pairs look at the completed list on the board and rate them from most helpful to least helpful. For example, if there are six items, have them rate them from 1 (most helpful) to 6 (least helpful).

5. Have pairs share their rankings and mark them on the board. Ask students to give reasons why one strategy might be more helpful than another. Make note of strategies that the majority feels are most helpful.

6. Finally, ask students: *If you can recognize a word when reading, but you cannot use it in writing, do you really "know" the word?* Give them time to think about the question and then elicit responses. Ask them which strategies can help them to better use new words in their writing, and add them to the list.

Multilevel Option 1

READING 1: You Can Read Faster and Better
A. VOCABULARY page 124

1. Ask a student to read the directions. Then give students time to do the activity. Remind them not to use their dictionaries during the activity.

2. Go over the answers with the class.

Background Note

READING 1 pages 125–126

In the past, reading comprehension was limited to a more discrete set of skills, including identifying main ideas, cause-effect relationships, comparisons and contrasts, and sequences of events. Today, however, cognitive psychology has expanded reading comprehension to "the construction of meaning," a much broader mental activity that is interactive, strategic, and adaptable. It's interactive in the sense that meaning is brought from the context and ideas of the text, as well as the reader's own personal experiences. It's strategic in that readers have different purposes for reading a particular text, which can affect the strategies they use to understand the text and their interpretation of it. It's adaptable because readers can utilize different strategies depending on the kind of text they are reading. For example, are they reading just to gather more information, or to support their own opinions?

"Good readers" are those who are selective and intentional. They make predictions about what they're going to read and focus their attention on the parts of the text that tie most closely to their reading goals. This means they may skip parts that aren't relevant to their research. "Good readers" also make inferences, meaning they're able to use their own background knowledge to "fill in the blanks" of a text when authors don't directly state ideas or associations between ideas. Finally, "good readers" are able to monitor their own reading comprehension. For example, if they are confused by the meaning of a key word in the text, they will identify the word, look it up, and then continue reading. Helping students acquire these skills, in addition to those mentioned in Reading 1, will greatly benefit them in becoming "faster and better" readers.

Multilevel Option 2

 WRITE WHAT YOU THINK page 128

1. Ask students to read the questions and reflect on their answers.

2. Seat students in small groups and assign roles: a group leader, a note-taker, a timekeeper, and a reporter.

3. Give students about five minutes to discuss the questions. Stop the conversations earlier if students are finishing sooner. Allow them an extra minute or two if necessary.

4. Call on each group's reporter to share ideas with the class.

5. Have each student choose one of the questions and write 5–8 sentences in response. This can be done in class or assigned as homework.

6. Call on volunteers to share their answers with the class.

MULTILEVEL OPTION

After students have selected a question, have them get into one of three groups according to the question they have chosen to answer. Then within each group, pair higher-level students with lower-level ones. Have the pairs write answers to the question. Encourage students to help each other. Each student should write out an answer.

Then have students compare and discuss their answers in their groups.

Background Note

READING 2 pages 132–133

In addition to the external influences on improved comprehension mentioned in Reading 2, including taking notes, studying in different places, and exercising, there is also research that shows people better comprehend information if it matches their natural learning style. For example, visual learners will better understand concepts if they are presented through pictures, graphs, videos, and written instructions. Auditory learners learn better through sound, meaning they would learn better by listening to a teacher's lecture than reading written notes. Kinesthetic learners are those who learn new concepts by "acting them out" through motions and physically-active activities. Finally, reading/writing learners are those who prefer reading about topics online or in books and then writing about them; they process information better through the written word than through visuals.

Expansion Activity 2

B. IDENTIFY page 134

1. Ask a student to read the directions. Then give students time to do the activity.

2. Go over the answers with the class.

3. Divide the class into three small groups. Ask each group to write a sentence that summarizes the main advice of the other three students from the reading (Ali, Sarah, and Alex). For a larger class, assign multiple groups to the same student from the reading. Assist the groups as necessary.

4. Write the headings "Ali", "Sarah", and "Alex" on the board. Have each group copy its main idea sentence on the board under the correct person/heading.

5. For classes with only three groups, have the class read and discuss the summary sentences. Have them discuss whether the sentences effectively summarize each student's advice, referring back to the text as necessary. For larger classes, have students compare the summary sentences from the different groups and decide which one best captures the main idea, and why.

Expansion Activity 3

WORK WITH THE VIDEO page 135

1. Tell students they will be creating a visual metaphor for an area of the brain discussed in the video. Explain: *A visual metaphor is like a symbol. It is an image or picture that that is used to compare one idea with another. The symbol is not literal. For example, a visual metaphor of the brain would not be a picture of a brain, but maybe a machine or a factory, suggesting that the brain works hard and "produces" our thoughts and behaviors.*

2. Divide the class into three groups. Assign each group a different area of the brain: *the brain stem, the cerebellum, and the cerebrum.*

3. Instruct each group to review their notes from Activity B on p. 135 and come up with a visual metaphor for their area of the brain and its main functions. If necessary, replay the video and have students take notes on the specific functions.

4. Give each group a piece of poster paper and a marker. Have them draw their visual metaphor on the poster. Tell them to title their posters after the area of the brain they have and write details around the image that explain how their area of the brain is like the image or symbol they chose (i.e., their reasons for the chosen image).

5. Have students put the posters up on the wall and give students time to walk around and read each one. Assign one person from each group as the poster representative. He or she will answer other students' questions about the poster as they walk around.

6. Have students put a checkmark on the poster they like the best, considering the metaphor chosen, the visual appeal, the organization, and the ideas.

7. Tally the votes and declare a winner. Ask those who selected the winning poster why they liked it. Keep the winning poster up on wall.

Vocabulary Skill Note

USING THE DICTIONARY page 136

1. Have a volunteer read the first paragraph. Then give students time to read the definitions. Explain: *When you look up a word, think about the context it is in. Think about the part of speech. This will help you choose the correct definition.*

2. Check comprehension by asking questions: *When are two definitions listed under the same word? When are two definitions put under different listings?*

Skill Note

It's important to help students understand that there are many kinds of dictionaries. A learner's dictionary is best suited to students and will provide helpful sample sentences. An electronic dictionary may provide just the definitions and pronunciation. Take time in the classroom to compare the information given in several different types of dictionaries.

Writing Skill Note

DESCRIBING A PROCESS page 139

1. Have volunteers read sections of the information.
2. Check comprehension: *Why do we use time order words? When do you need a comma after a time order word?*

Skill Note

Transitional words, such as the time order words mentioned here, are an important part of describing a process. They show the reader the sequence of events and they help to provide coherence and connection between sentences and paragraphs. Watch, however, that students do not overuse these words and expressions. Too many time order words, used too often, can make the writing seem mechanical.

Expansion Activity 4

B. IDENTIFY page 139

1. Read the directions. Give students time to do the activity.
2. To check their answers, have students read the steps in the correct order.

21ST CENTURY SKILLS EXPANSION

Oral and written communication skills are important for both consumers and employees in the 21st century. As consumers, and as users of technology, we often need to be able to explain the difficulties or problems in a process. To do this, we need to think critically to analyze the process and break it down into steps. These writing skills are highly valued in the workplace. In Reading 1, the author gives students tips and specific strategies on how to become a faster and more successful reader. In Reading 2, students discuss the specific steps they take to learn and study more effectively.

Multilevel Option 3

C. APPLY page 140

1. Read the directions and give students time to write the paragraph.
2. Have several students read their paragraphs. Remind students to use time order words and that there is more than one way to describe the process.

MULTILEVEL OPTION

Group lower-level students together and work with them to write the paragraph. You may wish to have students dictate it to you as you write on the board. Discuss any changes that need to be made. Then have students copy the paragraph from the board.

Have higher-level students complete the assignment individually. Then have students work in small groups or pairs to write another paragraph describing how to do something. When they are finished, ask for volunteers to read their descriptions.

Grammar Note

INFINITIVES OF PURPOSE page 141

1. Have volunteers read the information.
2. Check comprehension: *What is an* infinitive? *Is every infinitive an infinitive of purpose? How can you check to see if it is an infinitive of purpose?*
3. Write on the board: *Push the button to _____. She called me to _____.* Encourage students to use their imagination to make up sentences with these phrases. Have them share their sentences with the class.

Skill Note

Infinitives of purpose are very commonly used in textbook direction lines. Here are a few that you can point out to your students that are in the Unit Assignment section (Activities A–C), starting on page 143: *Use the chart* **to brainstorm** *ideas for a topic. Then make a list of time order words you can use* **to connect** *the steps of your process.*

Then use your notes from Activity B **to write** *your paragraph.*

As you go through activities, point out infinitives of purpose to your students.

Unit Assignment Rubrics

Unit 6   Brain Science

Unit Assignment Rubric

Student name: _____

Date: _____

Unit Assignment: *Write a paragraph describing a process that describes how you learn faster and better.*

20 points = Writing was completely successful (at least 90% of the time).
15 points = Writing was mostly successful (at least 70% of the time).
10 points = Writing was partially successful (at least 50% of the time).
 0 points = Writing was not successful.

Write a Paragraph Describing a Process	20 points	15 points	10 points	0 points
The topic sentence introduces the topic.				
The steps are clear and easy to understand.				
Time order words and connectors are used correctly.				
The paragraph has correct format and sentences have correct capitalization and punctuation.				
Infinitives of purpose are used correctly.				

Total points: _____

Comments:

Background Note

UNIT OPENER   pages 146–147

The photo on pp. 146–147 shows a pedestrian walkway in a park in the city of Suzhou City, China. Many flowers and bushes line the walkway. There are several modern, glass skyscrapers in the background. To the left is a large Ferris wheel.

Expansion Activity 1

UNIT QUESTION   page 147

1. Ask students: *How can nature affect how people in cities feel and behave? In other words, how do people feel when cities have a lot of nature around them, and what kinds of activities do they do in nature?*

2. Put students in small groups and give each group a piece of poster paper and a marker. On their paper, have them draw a T-chart. Tell them to label the left column *Feelings in nature* and the right column *Behavior in nature*. Have students brainstorm effects of nature on people's feelings and behavior.

3. Bring two students up to the board to be "note-takers." One student will take notes on *Feelings in nature* and the other on *Behavior in nature*. Ask each group to share their responses with the class and have the note-takers write their ideas under the corresponding titles on the board. Examples of feelings might include peaceful, calm, relaxed, energized, etc. Examples of behaviors might include walking, reading, relaxing, running, playing soccer, etc.

4. Ask the class if they believe it's important to have a lot of nature in cities, and why. Have them refer to the list on the board to help support their opinions.

5. Post the lists to refer back to later in the unit.

Multilevel Option 1

READING 1: Take a Nature Break
A. VOCABULARY   page 148

1. Ask a student to read the directions.
2. Have students complete the activity. Then go over the answers with the class.

MULTILEVEL OPTION

Group lower-level students and assist them with the task. Provide alternate example sentences to help them understand the words. *I'm **unable** to come to the party tomorrow because I have to work. I had many wonderful **experiences** when I visited my grandparents as a child. The company made a **generous** donation of $1 million to help the hurricane victims. Doing yoga **relaxes** my mind and body.*

Have higher-level students complete the activity individually and then compare answers with a partner. Have pairs write an additional example sentence for each word. Have volunteers write one of their sentences on the board. Correct the sentences with the whole class, focusing on the use of the expression rather than on other grammatical issues.

Background Note

READING 1   pages 149–150

In addition to more people living in cities, another major reason people today need more time in nature, according to experts, is because of how often people today are bombarded with electronic distractions, such as emails, social media, and phone notifications. Experts agree that the more time we spend on technology, the more the brain requires the healing properties of nature. The benefits are not just related to feeling more relaxed or less anxious, however. When people are too busy or distracted, it makes the brain work too hard, so it is harder to focus and think creatively. Research has shown that when people take nature breaks, they are more creative in their thinking, both during and afterwards, because their brain has been given time to wander, allowing new thoughts to surface.

Multilevel Option 2

WRITE WHAT YOU THINK   page 154

1. Ask students to read the questions and reflect on their answers.

2. Seat students in small groups and assign roles: a group leader to make sure everyone contributes, a note-taker to record the group's ideas, a timekeeper to watch the clock, and a reporter to share the group's ideas with the class.

3. Give students about five minutes to discuss the questions. Stop the conversations earlier if students are finishing sooner. Allow them an extra minute or two if necessary.

4. Call on each group's reporter to share ideas with the class.

5. Have each student choose one of the questions and write 5–8 sentences in response. This can be done in class or assigned as homework.

6. Call on volunteers to share their ideas with the class.

MULTILEVEL OPTION

After students have selected a question, have them get into one of three groups according to the question they have chosen. Then, within each group, pair higher-level students with lower-level ones. Have pairs write answers to the question. Encourage students to help each other. Each student should write out an answer. Then have students compare and discuss their answers in their groups.

Background Note

READING 2   pages 156–157

Currently, there is no established definition of what a "green city" is or should look like, but it is one that is generally believed to be sustainable and adhere to eco-friendly principles and practices, including reducing waste, increasing recycling programs, lowering pollution, expanding open green spaces, and supporting local, sustainable businesses. Green cities are also referred to as "sustainable cities" and "eco-cities". Green cities can be sustainable in a number of ways. Common approaches include using renewable energy sources, such as solar and wind, and developing comprehensive public transportation systems so fewer people are driving gasoline-powered cars on the roads, strategies that reduce a city's carbon footprint. Others include using electric-powered public busses, building more pedestrian walkways and cycling routes, constructing new buildings that are highly energy-efficient, and making older buildings more energy-efficient. Interestingly, urban areas can actually be more sustainable than rural and suburban areas due to their higher density. In cities, larger numbers of people and resources can be transported over shorter distances through public and mass transit systems, reducing demand for fossil fuels.

Expansion Activity 2

WORK WITH THE VIDEO page 160

1. As a class, review the advantages of urban farming mentioned in the video. Play the video a second time and have students take notes on the advantages.

2. Ask students to state the advantages and write them on the left side of the board under the title "Advantages". The advantages include: 1) growing healthy food closer to where most people live, 2) growing food you can find at local grocery stores, 3) using empty space to grow food people need, 4) providing more fresh food to local stores and restaurants, and 5) producing cleaner air.

3. Tell students: *In addition to advantages, solutions like urban farming can also have disadvantages. For example, one disadvantage of urban farming is that it can cost a lot of money to convert old buildings into ones that can sustain farming.* On the right side of the board, write the title "Disadvantages", and under it write, *expensive to convert old buildings*.

4. Tell students they will work in groups of four and brainstorm other disadvantages of urban farming to add to the list. Ask them to think about issues related to costs, convenience, safety, the environment, and labor.

5. Seat students in small groups and assign roles: a group leader to make sure everyone contributes, a note-taker to record the group's ideas, a reporter to share the group's ideas with the class, and a timekeeper to watch the clock. Give students 10–15 minutes to brainstorm their disadvantages.

6. Have each reporter share their group's disadvantages and write them under the "Disadvantages" title on the board, or have student volunteers write their ideas on the board.

7. Ask students to think about the advantages and disadvantages of urban farming in terms of the area where they live now. Ask: *Do you think urban farming would be a good solution for your city/town? Why or why not?*

8. Have students write a paragraph in response to the question. Encourage them to choose one side only and support their opinion with the advantages or disadvantages from the board. Collect the paragraphs and provide feedback on their ability to justify their opinion with specific reasons.

Expansion Activity 3

 ### WRITE WHAT YOU THINK
SYNTHESIZE page 161

1. Tell the students that they should think about the unit video, Reading 1, and Reading 2 as they answer the question. Students will write 5–8 sentences in response.

2. Give students about 8–10 minutes to write their answers. Encourage students to write freely without worrying about grammar.

3. Have each student compare their ideas with a partner. Give students a few minutes to discuss their ideas.

4. Have volunteers share their ideas with the class.

21ST CENTURY SKILLS EXPANSION

With the many environmental issues facing consumers and businesses in the 21st century, it is important to develop students' ability to think creatively and work cooperatively to solve problems.

A person who is aware of the consequences on the environment will be motivated to look for new solutions. In a business environment, employees often work collaboratively in order to come up with creative and innovation solutions to problems. A creative person will see a problem as an opportunity or a challenge.

Vocabulary Skill Note

PHRASAL VERBS page 161

1. Have volunteers read the information and examples.

2. Check comprehension by asking questions: *What is a phrasal verb? What is a separable phrasal verb?*

3. Ask volunteers to make up new sentences with the phrasal verbs. For sentences with separable phrasal verbs, have students give the sentences both ways.

Skill Note

A phrasal verb is usually a one-syllable verb followed by a particle. A particle looks like a preposition. When prepositions are used independently of verbs, they have clear and predictable meanings. But when these words follow certain verbs, they are called particles because they combine with the verb to make a phrasal verb with a unique meaning. For example, in the phrasal verb *pick up*, "up" does not carry the usual meaning of the preposition.

Grammar Note

SIMPLE PAST AND PAST CONTINUOUS page 163

1. Have volunteers read the information and examples.

2. Check comprehension by asking questions: *Which past tense do we use for a series of completed actions? Which tense do we use to emphasize the duration of an action? When do we use the two tenses together?*

3. Ask students to write a sentence using *when* or *while* with the past tense, or divide the class into two, with one writing a sentence with *when* and the other with *while*. Ask for volunteers to share their sentences and write them on the board. Make corrections as necessary.

Skill Note

The past continuous is often used to provide background information in a story, or to explain what events were happening before the main events, e.g., *I was sitting on my couch after dinner. The television was on, and I was watching a soccer game. All of a sudden, I heard a knock at the door. I wasn't expecting anyone, so I was a little surprised.* It can help students to think of the past continuous as actions that were in progress *before* the main event, and actions that were happening together at the same time.

Writing Skill Note

USING SENTENCE VARIETY page 164

1. Call on volunteers to read sections of the information.

2. Check comprehension: *Why is sentence variety important? Do you use long sentences in your writing? How often do you use questions and imperatives? Do you think that sentence variety will help your score on an essay test? Why?*

Skill Note

Sentence variety is an important concept to introduce and reinforce. Students are capable of using long and short sentences, questions, and imperatives. They should check every piece of writing for sentence variety during the editing process. In academic writing courses and in standardized tests with writing sections, sentence variety is a component of most grading rubrics.

Unit Assignment Rubrics

Unit 7   Environmental Science

Unit Assignment Rubric

Student name: _____

Date: _____

Unit Assignment: *Write a paragraph that states and supports your opinion.*

20 points = Writing was completely successful (at least 90% of the time).
15 points = Writing was mostly successful (at least 70% of the time).
10 points = Writing was partially successful (at least 50% of the time).
 0 points = Writing was not successful.

Write an Opinion Paragraph	20 points	15 points	10 points	0 points
The paragraph clearly states the writer's opinion about the topic.				
There are at least two reasons given to support the opinion.				
The writer provides facts to support the reasons.				
There is sentence variety.				
The simple past and past continuous are used correctly.				

Total points: _____

Comments:

Background Note

UNIT OPENER   pages 170–171

The photo on pp. 170–171 shows an Asian boy in a city playground in Taiwan. He is sitting on a rocking horse. He is wearing a mask to protect himself from air pollution.

Expansion Activity 1

UNIT QUESTION   page 171

1. Put students in small groups and give each group a piece of poster paper and a marker.

2. Read the Unit Question aloud: *How can we prevent diseases?* Give students a minute to silently consider their answers to the Unit Question. Tell students to pass the paper and the marker around the group. Direct each group member to write a different answer to the question. Encourage students to help one another.

3. Ask each group to choose a reporter to read the answers to the class. Point out similarities and differences among the answers. If answers from different groups are similar, make a group list that incorporates all of the answers. Post the list to refer back to later in the unit.

Background Note

READING 1   pages 173–174

The Internet is now a popular source for information about medical conditions and health problems. People find it easy to search for and find information on the web. Many websites have FAQs (pronounced like *fax*) pages similar to this one. Other websites have information divided into categories such as topic overview, causes, symptoms, treatment, exams and tests, prevention, medications, and so on.

Reading Skill Note

SYNTHESIZING INFORMATION   page 177

1. Have volunteers read the information aloud. Go over the diagram orally. Explain: *When we use this book, we usually synthesize information from Reading 1 and Reading 2. Synthesis questions require you to think deeply. They are common in essay test questions.*

2. Check comprehension by asking questions: *What kinds of information can you synthesize? Why is it good to use information from various sources when you do research?*

Skill Note

Synthesizing information is considered to be a high-level critical thinking skill. In this text, students continually have to synthesize information as they analyze and discuss the readings. Discussion questions are designed to push students to think more deeply and make connections between what they know and

what they are learning. In academic courses, many assignments and test questions require students to synthesize information. In the classroom, encourage students to use what they already know when they answer questions. Ask them what else they have learned about the topic and where they learned the information.

Multilevel Option 1

B. SYNTHESIZE   page 178

1. Read the directions and the two questions. Explain that these types of questions are similar to ones they may have on a test in a science class.

2. Give students five minutes to write their answers. Remind them to use complete sentences.

3. Go over the answers orally.

MULTILEVEL OPTION

Group lower-level students together and work with them to do the activity. Start by having a volunteer read the paragraph aloud. Explain that to answer the questions, they have to think about what they already learned about the seasonal flu. For question 1, have them discuss sample answers. For question 2, see what students might already know about how the avian flu has spread in the past. Then give students time to write their answers individually.

For higher-level students, have students discuss sample answers in small groups. Then have students write their answers individually.

Expansion Activity 2

READING 2: Preventing Disease around the World
A. VOCABULARY   page 179

1. Ask a student to read the directions. Then give students time to do the activity. Remind them not to use their dictionaries during the activity.

2. Go over the answers with the class.

Expand Vocabulary

1. Have students use their dictionaries to find additional meanings for the following words: *risk, treat, volunteer.* Explain: *Some words use the same forms for both nouns and verbs, so you may need to look at the context closely to determine a word's part of speech.* Have students look up each of these words and write down the definitions for the verb meaning and the noun meaning. Then students write an example sentence for each.

2. Give students about ten minutes to look up the words and complete the task.

3. Call on volunteers to read their words and sentences. Ask: *Did the words have more meanings as nouns or as verbs? Which word had the most meanings?*

Background Note

READING 2 pages 180–181

Today, there are many non-profit organizations whose goal is to reduce the number of infectious diseases around the world. Some of the biggest global health concerns, particularly in poorer countries, include HIV/AIDS, cholera, tuberculosis, and malaria. Many infectious diseases, such as tuberculosis and measles, are preventable through routine vaccinations. Others, such as HIV and cholera, are preventable through adequate education, such as teaching people ways to practice safe sex, and how to sanitize dirty water. Many poorer countries often do not have the resources to prevent infectious diseases, either through vaccinations or through public health education. One of the biggest players in the fight against infectious diseases worldwide is the World Health Organization (WHO), who work with partners, such as the Bill and Melinda Gates Foundation, to provide the medical care and resources required to combat global health issues.

Multilevel Option 2

G. APPLY page 183

1. Ask a volunteer to read the directions. Review what kinds of information a summary should and should not include.

2. Give students 10-15 minutes to write their summaries. Remind them to use complete sentences.

3. Ask volunteers to write their summaries on the board. Provide feedback as necessary.

MULTILEVEL OPTION

Group lower-level students in pairs. Assign just one paragraph to each pair (para. 3, 4, or 6). Circulate and provide help as necessary. Help students identify the main topic of the paragraph they are summarizing before they write their two-sentence summaries.

For higher-level students, have students work individually to write two-sentences summaries for all three paragraphs. Then have them compare their summaries with a partner.

Expansion Activity 3

WORK WITH THE VIDEO page 184

1. Explain to students that a *myth* is a belief that many people have but is not true. Tell them that many people have myths about what causes colds, how colds are spread, and how to treat colds. For example, in the United States, many people believe having hot chicken soup can help cure a cold.

2. Have students identify which of the experiments from the video tried to disprove a myth. (Experiment 1: You can catch a cold from being cold.)

3. Put students into groups and have them brainstorm other common myths about colds. Have them think about myths they've read about, or ones that people in their family or their culture believe about preventing or curing colds. Give them 10–15 minutes to discuss.

4. As students are working in groups, write the headings *What causes colds*, *How colds are spread*, and *How to treat colds* on the board.

5. Call time and have a member from each group write their myths under the correct heading on the board. Offer help as necessary.

6. Review the myths and ask students where they learned about the myth. Is it a cultural belief? Is it an old myth? Did they learn it from someone in their family? Has it been passed down from previous generations? Did they read about it somewhere?

7. Ask students to work in their groups to create an experiment that could prove or disprove one of the myths. Have them write down the question they're trying to answer, and what steps they would take to test the myth.

8. Have each group present their ideas for experiments to the class. Ask the class what challenges the group might face in doing the experiment in real-life.

Expansion Activity 4

WRITE WHAT YOU THINK
SYNTHESIZE page 185

1. Ask students to read the questions and reflect on their answers.

2. Seat students in small groups and assign roles: a group leader to make sure everyone contributes, a note-taker to record the group's ideas, a reporter to share the group's ideas with the class, and a timekeeper to watch the clock.

3. Give students about ten minutes to discuss the questions.

4. Ask a few students to share their answers with the class.

21ST CENTURY SKILLS EXPANSION

In the 21st century, collaboration and creativity are vital in our ever-changing global economy. This reading provides an example of how medical experts collaborate with non-profit organizations to solve problems in global health. For example, in this reading, Dr. Andersson-Swayze worked with the International Medical Corps to stop the spread of Ebola in West Africa. In students' academic careers, they will often need to collaborate with other students to do projects or conduct research. Thinking creatively will often lead to new ways of thinking about problems and solutions. In the workplace, collaboration is extremely important and is an integral part of most jobs. Creative thinkers can see new approaches to questions and issues in the workplace.

Vocabulary Skill Note

COLLOCATIONS page 185

1. Have a volunteer read the information aloud.

2. Check comprehension by asking questions: *What is a collocation? Why do you think it is helpful to learn these collocations?*

Skill Note

There are many different types of collocations. Phrases such as the ones presented in the student book are very common. (Note that a verb + a preposition combination does not always result in a phrasal verb. With phrasal verbs, the addition of a particle changes the meaning of the verb, e.g., *drop* vs. *drop by*. With these verb phrases, the meaning of the verb doesn't change with the addition of a preposition.) A collocation can also be two words that are often used together, such as *severe cold* or *symptoms include*. Idioms are considered collocations. Two examples are *go with the flow* and *twist someone's arm*. Since collocations are hard to predict and often don't follow a pattern, they are challenging for language learners. Tell students that any time they learn a new word they should pay attention to the words surrounding it.

Writing Skill Note

WRITING AN EXPLANATORY PARAGRAPH page 187

1. Have volunteers read sections of the information aloud.

2. Check comprehension. Ask: *Why do we use explanatory paragraphs? In what types of readings would you find an explanatory paragraph?*

Skill Note

While the skill presentation gives several guidelines for writing an explanatory paragraph, the activities that follow will likely result in students writing paragraphs that simply explain the term and give examples. Encourage students to consider writing about how a term is different from similar terms or writing about what the term or concept is not. For example, in Activity D, students could compare one disease with another, such as comparing the common cold with allergies or the flu. They could make a Venn diagram and list everything they know about the two diseases. Then they could use some of the information in their explanatory paragraph in Activity E.

Grammar Note

ADVERBS OF MANNER AND DEGREE page 190

1. Have volunteers read the information.

2. Check comprehension: *What is an* adverb of manner? *What is an* adverb of degree? *Do they always come after verbs?*

Skill Note

Most adverbs of manner end in *-ly*; the most common exceptions *are fast, slow,* and *hard*. Students often make mistakes by placing the adverb between the verb and the object (*You play well soccer* should be *You play soccer well.*).

Multilevel Option 3

B. PLAN page 192

1. Read the directions and the questions aloud. Remind students to think of the purpose of a FAQ page about an illness: to answer the most typical questions that a person might have about the illness.

2. Give students ten minutes to answer the questions. You may want to assign this as homework.

3. Have students share answers and ideas with a partner. You may pair students who have the same topics.

MULTILEVEL OPTION

Put lower-level students in groups of three or four and assist them with the task. Have each group choose a different topic. Each group will write a FAQ page. Select a few higher-level students to work with the groups. Have the students share information and ideas to answer the questions. Have the rest of the higher-level students work individually to plan their FAQ pages. If possible, have them research the topics online to find additional information.

Unit Assignment Rubrics

Unit 8   Public Health

Unit Assignment Rubric

Student name: _____

Date: _____

Unit Assignment: *Write an FAQ page about an illness that includes a definition of your topic.*

20 points = Writing was completely successful (at least 90% of the time).
15 points = Writing was mostly successful (at least 70% of the time).
10 points = Writing was partially successful (at least 50% of the time).
 0 points = Writing was not successful.

Create an FAQ Page	20 points	15 points	10 points	0 points
The defining paragraph is clear and easy to understand.				
Each response directly answers the question.				
Each sentence has correct capitalization and punctuation.				
Sentences use natural collocations.				
The writer correctly used at least one adverb of manner and one adverb of degree.				

Total points: _____

Comments:

Student Book Answer Key

Unit-by-Unit detailed Student Book Answer Key.

The Q Classroom
Activity A., p. 3
1. Answers will vary.
2. Answers will vary. These people are reporters at a promotional event for a new smartphone model. A new product is exciting when it offers something you had not seen before.

Activity B., p. 3
1. Answers will vary. Possible answers: Yes, I think that is true. / No, I do not think that is true.
2. Answers will vary. Possible answer: Some things become popular because they are new and different.

READING 1
PREVIEW THE READING
Activity A., p. 4
1. find out
2. trend
3. spread
4. contribute
5. connect
6. express
7. clear

Activity B., p. 5
Answers will vary. The article will talk about unusual things that advertisers do to promote products.

Activity C., p. 5
Answers will vary.

WORK WITH THE READING
Activity B., p. 6
1. c
2. d
3. a
4. b

Activity C., p. 6
a. 4 This created buzz because people like to participate and express their own opinions.
b. 3 Some other companies choose to do something surprising so that people will remember their product and spread their idea.
c. 1 Every year companies spend millions of dollars on advertising to create buzz about their products—in other words, to get people talking about them.
d. 6 There are many ways that advertisers hope to make their products popular: doing something surprising or exciting, asking customers to get involved, or connecting the product with something that people see regularly.
e. 2 This is part of a new trend in advertising, in which companies pay for unusual events, hoping that customers will talk more about their products.
f. 3 People were surprised to see a blender cut a smartphone into small pieces. Everyone talked about the videos and wanted to find out more about the blenders.

Activity D., p. 7
1. *Buzz* means "people talk a lot about something because it is popular."
2. 39 kilometers
3. more than 1,300 kilometers per hour
4. smartphones, rakes, sports equipment
5. They connected Kit Kat™ bars with coffee.

6. Sales improved by more than 50 percent.
7. Because more people will buy products that people are talking about.

Activity E., p. 7
1. Felix Baumgartner performed a stunt while wearing a space suit with Red Bull™'s name on it. (Par. 2)
2. Tom Dickson made videos showing blenders mixing up unusual things. (Par. 3)
3. Doritos™ asked their customers to make their own TV ads. (Par. 4)
4. they drink coffee often, and the ads connected Kit Kat™s with coffee. (Par. 5)

WRITE WHAT YOU THINK
Activity A., B., pp. 7–8
1. Answers will vary. Sample answer: I think Kit Kat™ had the most successful advertising method. They improved sales by more than 50 percent because they used ads that connected Kit Kat™ bars with coffee.
2. Answers will vary.

READING SKILL
Activity A., p. 8
1. Experts often influence our actions and purchases.
2. Other consumers also influence our purchases.

Activity B., pp. 8–9
1. c Key sentence: *One idea that can contribute to popularity is to do something very unusual.*
2. a Key sentence: *Some other companies choose to do something surprising so that people will remember their product and spread their idea.*
3. c Key sentence: *This created buzz because people like to participate and express their own opinions.*
4. b Key sentence: *Another way to make a product popular is to connect it in people's minds with something that they see often.*

READING 2
PREVIEW THE READING
Activity A., pp. 9–10
1. a
2. b
3. b
4. a
5. a
6. a
7. b
8. b

Activity B., p. 10
☑ People make their shopping choices because of what other people buy.

Activity C., p. 10
Answers will vary. Sample answer: I bought a pair of expensive sneakers because all my friends had the same pair. I liked the way the sneakers looked, but they were expensive. I wish I had saved my money instead.

WORK WITH THE READING
Activity B., p. 12
1. a
2. b

Activity C., pp. 12–13
1. Par. 2; Social proof is how other people's actions influence us.
2. Par. 3; They want to influence us to buy their products.
3. Par. 3; because experts are knowledgeable
4. Par. 4; People are interested in consumers' opinions.
5. Par. 6; a friend's recommendations

Activity D., p. 13
Answers will vary.

Activity E., p. 14
1. influence
2. behavior
3. Experts
4. consumers
5. friends
6. recommendations
7. advertising

Activity F., p. 14
- ☑ 1
- ☑ 3
- ☑ 4
- ☑ 6

Activity G., p. 14
Answers will vary.

WORK WITH THE VIDEO
Activity B., C., p. 15
Answers will vary.

WRITE WHAT YOU THINK
p. 16
Answers will vary.

VOCABULARY SKILL
Activity A., p. 16
Nouns: choice, connection, contribution, discussion, enjoyment, gift, information, thought
Verbs: choose, connect, contribute, discuss, enjoy, give, inform, think

Activity B., p. 17
1. V
2. N
3. V
4. N
5. N
6. V
7. N
8. V
9. V
10. N

Activity C., p. 17
1. studies
2. reviews
3. influence
4. comments
5. researches
6. study
7. comments
8. influence

WRITING SKILL
Activity A., p. 18
TS Psychologists say that "social proof" influences us.
SS One example of this is a sidewalk experiment.

SS When a group of four people looked up at the sky on a busy sidewalk, 80% of the passersby looked up also.
CS A group of people influences the behavior of others.

Activity B., p. 19
1. b
2. c
3. a

Activity C., p. 19
Topic sentence: *Friends influence us the most—more than experts, crowds, or other consumers.*

Activity D., p. 19
1. b topic: the most popular clothing / controlling idea: is not always popular the next year
2. c topic: classroom computers / controlling idea: are very helpful for students
3. a topic: many older adults / controlling idea: need a lesson on how to use a smartphone

Activity E., pp. 19–20
1. b
2. b

Activity F., p. 20
Answers will vary. Possible answer: I have good reasons for not buying the latest fashions.

Activity G., p. 20
Answers will vary.

Activity H., p. 21
Answers will vary.

GRAMMAR
Activity A., p. 22
1. Nowadays more and more companies <u>are making</u> advertisements that involve their customers. These companies <u>are using</u> many creative ways to help products become more popular. Researchers believe social proof is the idea behind this trend. This is because when we are not sure what to do, we look at what others <u>are doing</u>. More and more people <u>are using</u> smartphones and social media to share news about their purchases with their friends.
2. a
3. c

Activity B., p. 22
1. are using
2. are following
3. are copying
4. are buying
5. are complaining
6. is spreading
7. is improving
8. are losing
9. are being

UNIT ASSIGNMENT
PLAN AND WRITE
Activity A., p. 23
Answers will vary.

Activity B., p. 23
Answers will vary.

The Q Classroom
Activity A., p. 27
Answers will vary. Possible answers:
1. I like blue because it is easy to look at. It's a calm color. It's easy to match blue with other colors.
2. Yellow walls will probably make me feel warm and happy. It's a cheerful color.
3. The color makes the room appear bright and the woman friendly. Dark walls and clothes would make the woman appear more serious.

Activity B., p. 27
1. The students mention bright colors, burgundy, dark blue, gold, white, and pink.
2. Answers will vary.

READING 1
PREVIEW THE READING
Activity A., pp. 28–29
a. represent
b. affect
c. variety
d. culture
e. universal
f. unaware
g. psychology
h. character

Activity B., p. 29
Answers will vary. Possible answers:
1. Colors and clothing.
2. There are three photos. The captions describe how the people in the photos feel about wearing certain colors.
3. Green makes her think about nature.
4. Colors can affect people in different ways.

Activity C., p. 29
Answers will vary. Possible answer: The color red makes me feel happy. Red is a warm color and makes me feel safe. When I think of the color red, I am reminded of leaves in the fall.

WORK WITH THE READING
Activity B., p. 31
1. T
2. F, Paragraph 2. They are serious and intelligent.
3. T
4. F, Paragraph 4. They are cheerful.
5. T

Activity C., p. 32
blue: confident, reliable, calm, peacefulness
yellow: happiness, sun, laughter, creativity
green: good mood, peace, happiness, active, good with money, caring, kind
white: something new, neat, organized, goodness, death

Activity D., p. 32
Answers will vary. Possible answers:
1. Most people think carefully about color.
2. According to research, black suggests that you are serious and intelligent.
3. Blue gives a feeling of calm and peacefulness.
4. Yellow clothing is often used by active, creative people.
5. Scientists say that the color green gives you a good mood.
6. Colors may have different meanings in different cultures.

Activity E., pp. 32–33
Answers will vary. Possible answers:
1. The colors you choose can tell us something about you.
2. The color black suggests that you are serious and intelligent.
3. Yellow makes you feel happier.
4. People wear white when they are starting something new.
5. Colors may have different meanings in different cultures.
6. Colors can affect people in different ways.

WRITE WHAT YOU THINK
Activity A., B., p. 33
Answers will vary. Possible answers:
1. I like to wear blue. I think it makes me look more reliable.
2. My bedroom walls are white, so my walls look clean and my bedroom looks large. I like white because I can decorate my walls with posters of any color. I can use any color for my bed. Someday I would like to change the color to yellow. Yellow is a warm and cheerful color.

READING SKILL
Activity A., p. 34
The following should be circled:
1. different
2. trees, flowers, grass
3. university students, long, black, graduate
4. worn, police officers
5. good, parents, workers, depend on
6. variety, light, dark

Activity B., p. 34
Answers will vary. Sample answers:
1. a lot of different things
2. the plants and animals in the world
3. a long, loose piece of clothing, sometimes worn on special occasions
4. special clothes that people at the same job or on the same team wear
5. dependable; that you can trust
6. how light or dark a color is

READING 2
PREVIEW THE READING
Activity A., p. 35
1. c
2. a
3. c
4. a
5. b
6. a
7. b
8. b

Activity B., p. 35
McDonalds, Microsoft, Dell, Apple, BP, UPS

Activity C., p. 35
Answers will vary.

WORK WITH THE READING

Activity B., p. 37
☑ 2

Activity C., p. 37

Name of company	Company colors	Feelings that colors give
McDonald's	red and yellow	bright, cheerful
Microsoft, Dell	blue	dependable, peaceful, powerful
Apple	variety of colors	fun
BP	green and yellow	nature, sun, energy, bright, cheerful, environmentally friendly
UPS	brown	safe, reliable, boring, dependable

Activity D., p. 37
Answers will vary. Sample answers:
1. McDonald's uses red and yellow because they are bright and cheerful colors.
2. The UPS color is brown. It represents safe and reliable service.
3. Computer companies use blue to show that they are dependable and powerful.
4. BP's green and yellow represent the environment and are bright and cheerful.

Activity E., p. 38
Answers will vary. Possible answers:
1. Scientists have indicated that you feel happier around the color yellow.
2. When people choose clothing, they think carefully about color.
3. People who are usually happy and like different things often wear orange.
4. Few colors mean the same thing to everyone.
5. You might think that the color brown is not an interesting color for a company.

Activity F., pp. 38–39
1. cheerful
2. reliable
3. positive
4. products
5. respond

WORK WITH THE VIDEO
Activity A., p. 39
Answers will vary.

Activity B., p. 39
1. b
2. a
3. c
4. a

Activity C, p. 39
Answers will vary.

WRITE WHAT YOU THINK
Synthesize, p. 40
Answers will vary. Possible answers:
1. McDonald's uses red and yellow, which are bright and cheerful colors. They use red and yellow on all of their cups and packages and in their advertising. When I drive, I can recognize a McDonald's restaurant from the colors. UPS uses

brown. Brown is not a lively color. It makes me think the company is slow. Many computer companies use blue. I think blue is a very serious color. It makes me feel confident in the companies.
2. I would use green and blue for the shelves to create a relaxing environment for the children. The tables and reading area will be red and yellow, so that they look inviting and children will want to sit and read at them. The walls would be white so that the room is not too distracting.

VOCABULARY SKILL
Activity A., pp. 40–41
1. N
2. ADJ
3. ADJ
4. N
5. N
6. ADJ
7. ADJ
8. N

Activity B., p. 41
1. addition
2. environmental
3. natural
4. peace
5. person

Activity C., p. 41
1. nature
2. peaceful
3. person
4. environment
5. additional

WRITING SKILL
Activity A., p. 42
Answers will vary.

Activity B., p. 43
Answers will vary. Sample answer:
Topic: Think of a national flag. What are the main colors in the flag? What does each color represent?

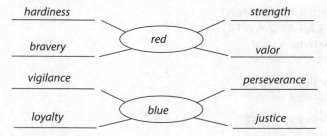

Activity C., p. 43
Companies and colors, Internet companies—Google uses lots of different colors, they are bright, happy colors—Amazon uses mostly black and yellow I think. I wonder why they picked those colors. ~~My brother bought a backpack on Amazon. He takes it to school every day.~~ Stores—Macy's department store uses red. I like the color red. It's a strong, exciting color. Macy's uses a red star in its advertisements.
I always think of the red star and Macy's. ~~Sometimes I shop at Macy's.~~ The red star is a good symbol. It's easy to remember and recognize.

Activity D., p. 43
Underline: Stores—Macy's department store uses red. I like the color red. It's a strong, exciting color. Macy's uses a red star in its advertisements. I always think of the red star and Macy's. The red star is a good symbol. It's easy to remember and recognize.

Activity E., pp. 43–44
Answers will vary.

Activity F., p. 44
Answers will vary.

GRAMMAR
Activity A., p. 45
1. will be
2. will encourage
3. will use
4. will, go
5. will, be
6. will love
7. will enjoy
8. will bring
9. will, use
10. will have
11. will offer

Activity B., p. 45

	Example	Reason
1. simple present	introduce	It happens every year.
2. simple past	announced	It happened last week.
3. future with *will*	will be	Next year is the future.

Activity C., p. 46
Answers will vary. Sample answers:
1. My city will have more people living in it in 50 years.
2. The buses in my town will move faster.
3. Stores will be larger and have more items to choose from.
4. There will be more pollution and fewer trees in my town.
5. I will be older.
6. I will have children and grandchildren.
7. I will be retired.

UNIT ASSIGNMENT
PLAN AND WRITE
Activity A., p. 47
Answers will vary.

Activity B., p. 47
Answers will vary.

Activity C., p. 47
Answers will vary.

The Q Classroom
Activity A., p. 51
Answers will vary. Possible answers:
1. I invited several friends to come for dinner. I spent hours making a delicious meal. Only one friend came. The other friends never called to tell me they couldn't come. I didn't invite them for dinner again.
2. The woman is throwing a plastic bottle out the window of her moving car. She clearly doesn't care about the environment or others.

Activity B., p. 51
1. Saying *thank you, please*, and *excuse me*. Don't interrupt people. Don't ask personal questions. Smile. Eat slowly. Don't be messy.
2. Answers will vary.

READING 1
PREVIEW THE READING
Activity A., p. 52
a. respect
b. behavior
c. awkward
d. make a good impression
e. firmly
f. manners
g. appropriately
h. gesture

Activity B., p. 53
The photos and captions suggest that this article will be about manners such as shaking hands, using eye contact, and giving gifts in different cultures.

Activity C., p. 53
Answers will vary.

WORK WITH THE READING
Activity B., pp. 54–55
1. F, Paragraph 1. Polite behavior is often different in different countries.
2. T, Paragraph 3
3. F, Paragraph 4. Personal space is different in different cultures.
4. F, Paragraph 6. Each country has a different definition of being on time.
5. T, Paragraph 7
6. F, Paragraph 8. It is useful to learn about cultural differences.

Activity C., p. 55
1. b
2. a
3. c
4. b
5. b
6. a

Activity D., p. 56

Paragraph number	Country or region	Topic
2	United States, Middle Eastern countries	greetings
4	North America, Middle East, Latin America	personal space
5	United States, China	gift-giving
6	Germany, Argentina	time
7	Vietnam, United States	gestures

Activity E., p. 56
Answers will vary. Possible answers:
1. Examples differ from culture to culture. In the United States, it is polite to shake hands firmly and to open a gift when it is given to you.
2. In the United States, people shake hands firmly and for a short period of time. In the Middle East, people shake hands gently and for a longer time.
3. In North America, the comfortable distance is at arm's length. Where I live, we stand closer together.
4. It shows that you care about the other person and want to make that person feel comfortable. If you are in another country, it shows that you respect the other person's culture.

WRITE WHAT YOU THINK
Activity A., p. 56
Answers will vary. Possible answers:
1. In my culture, we don't touch strangers in public spaces. For example, on a train, you only touch someone if you have to. At school, we stand about 24 inches apart when we are talking. In the office, people usually stand a little further apart.
2. Children learn to be polite by watching what others do, especially their parents. However, it is really important for parents to teach a child manners from an early age. Children also learn about politeness from teachers and by interaction with other children.

Activity B., p. 57
Answers will vary.

READING SKILL
Activity A., p. 57
Main Idea: There are cultural differences in the way people use personal space.
Detail: In North America, people usually stand about an arm's length apart during a conversation.
Detail: in some countries in the Middle East and Latin America, people stand closer.

Activity B., p. 57
1. Around the world cultures have different ideas about giving gifts.
2. There are two supporting details: In the United States, if people give you a gift, you should open it while they are with you... In China, you should open a gift after the person is gone.

Activity C., p. 58
1. Another cultural difference is time.
2. In Germany, it is important to arrive on time. In Argentina, polite dinner guests usually come 30 to 60 minutes after the time of the invitation.

READING 2
PREVIEW THE READING
Activity A., pp. 58–59
1. c
2. a
3. a
4. b
5. b
6. c
7. a
8. c

Activity B., p. 59
Answers will vary. Possible other topics: formality; when to leave a tip; appropriate work clothing

Activity C., p. 59
Answers will vary.

WORK WITH THE READING
Activity B., p. 61
Answers may vary. Sample corrections:
1. Yong Jun Park's host will probably <u>not</u> talk about business during dinner. Name: <u>Andrea</u>
2. It is appropriate to bring a <u>small</u> gift when visiting a home in the U.S. Name: <u>Sue</u>
3. <u>Most</u> Americans are <u>informal</u> at home. Name: <u>Jun</u>
4. <u>In the U.S.,</u> it is rude to come in and interrupt a business meeting. Name: <u>Carlos</u>

Activity C., pp. 61–62
1. **a.** later
   b. right away
2. **a.** travel, food, books, sports, family
   b. age, salary, religion, politics
3. **a.** discuss business
   b. have informal conversation before a meeting
4. **a.** are acceptable
   b. are unacceptable

Activity D., p. 62
1. manners
2. informal
3. kitchen
4. polite
5. hosts
6. left
7. conversation
8. relationships
9. interrupt

Activity E., p. 63
Answers will vary. Possible answers:
1. Good table manners in the United States include keeping elbows off the table; chewing with your mouth closed; complimenting the food.
2. It is important to make your guests feel comfortable, but it is also important for visitors to learn about your culture. You can explain customs to them so that they understand.

WORK WITH THE VIDEO
Activity A., p. 63
Answers will vary.

Activity B., p. 63
1. F
2. T
3. F
4. F
5. T

Activity C., p. 63
1. Answers will vary. Possible answers: It is unacceptable to use a mobile phone at the theater or movie theater, or in class. It is acceptable to use a mobile phone in a restaurant or café.
2. Answers will vary.

WRITE WHAT YOU THINK
Synthesize, p. 64
Answers will vary. Possible answers:
1. I think that people are less polite today. This is because they are not taught how to be polite from a young age. People are less formal now. They are less respectful of older people.
2. People learn to be polite. As children, we are only interested in ourselves. Parents and teachers teach us manners. This is one reason why there are different customs around the world.

VOCABULARY SKILL
Activity A., p. 64
in-: inappropriate, inexpensive, informal
im-: imperfect, impolite, impossible
un-: unclear, uncomfortable, uncommon, undependable, untraditional, unusual

Activity B., p. 65
1. dependable
2. unclear
3. unusual OR uncommon
4. impossible
5. comfortable
6. inexpensive
7. impolite OR inappropriate
8. traditional OR formal
9. uncomfortable
10. inappropriate OR impolite

WRITING SKILL
Activity A., p. 66
Circled: there are several appropriate gifts to bring to a host
Underlined: flowers, Food, a small gift for the home
Highlighted: For example, For instance

Activity B., pp. 66–67
1. in North America, people stand an arm's length apart. In some countries in the Middle East and Latin America, people stand closer.
2. in some Middle Eastern countries, people hold the other person's hand gently for a longer time.
3. it is polite to be half an hour to an hour late in Argentina.
4. in the United States, it is polite for hosts to open a gift in front of the gift giver.
5. it is impolite to interrupt a meeting in the United States, but it is common for others to come in the room in Egypt.

Activity C., p. 67
Answers will vary. Sample answer:
Main idea: Many people are impolite when using their cell phones.
Supporting idea: People speak loudly in public places.
Supporting idea: People use their phones at dinner.
Supporting idea: People interrupt conversations to answer their cell phones.

Activity D., p. 67
Answers will vary. Sample answer:
Many people do not have good cell phone manners, and they are impolite when they use their cell phones. For example, some people speak loudly on the phone in public places, such as the movie theater or on the bus. When eating dinner with friends or family, impolite people may have their cell phones out and play games or read text messages rather than focus on the dinner conversation. Other impolite people interrupt conversations to answer their cell phones. Instead, they should allow their calls to go to voicemail, and answer them later. This way they can focus on the conversation. If cell phone users were more thoughtful of others, they might be more polite.

Activity E., p. 68
Answers will vary.

Activity F., p. 68
Answers will vary.

GRAMMAR
Activity A., p. 69
1. Circled: brother
lives
2. Circled: a man
is
3. Circled: The police
are
4. Circled: People
use
5. Circled: This book
gives

Activity B., p. 70
In my opinion, the most annoying (habit) is talking on cell phones. (People) is talking talk on their cell phones all the time. My (brother) always interrupt interrupts our conversations and answer answers his phone. (People) like my brother doesn't don't care about manners. (People) talk on cell phones in restaurants and in doctors' offices. There is are (times) when (cell phones) are very annoying. (Cell phones) ring and interrupts interrupt our thoughts. (People) need to show more respect for others. There is are appropriate and inappropriate (places) to use cell phones.

UNIT ASSIGNMENT
PLAN AND WRITE
Activity A., p. 70
Answers will vary.

PLAN
Activity B., p. 71
Answers will vary.

WRITE
Activity C., p. 71
Answers will vary.

The Q Classroom
Activity A., p. 75
1. Answers will vary. Possible answers: I use a cell phone, a laptop, and the Internet every day. My laptop and the Internet improve my performance by making it easier to write things and do research.
2. Answers will vary. Possible answers: The girl is at a technology fair. She is testing some kind of virtual reality device.

Activity B., p. 75
1. Vocabulary app, music software, running software, video software
2. Answers will vary. Students may mention fitness software, pronunciation software, calendar software for tracking activities, and so on.

READING 1
PREVIEW THE READING
Activity A., p. 76
a. specific
b. replace
c. technology
d. examine
e. situation
f. take care of
g. performance
h. under pressure

Activity B., p. 77
Answers will vary.

Activity C., p. 77
Answers will vary. Possible answers: List of technology could include: computer applications of various types; videotaping; audio books; audio recording; virtual reality; games for learning

WORK WITH THE READING
Activity B., p. 79
2

Activity C., p. 79
1. b
2. a
3. b
4. a
5. c

Activity D., p. 80
1. VR can help a student understand how bones and muscles are connected. It can help students see under different layers.
2. Using VR for examinations helps a student learn what to do and practice before helping a real patient. With VR, the student can learn what they need to improve.
3. Possible answers: Yes, it is good because it is similar to a real situation and the student has to make decisions quickly. / No, it cannot replace the real experience.

Activity E., p. 80
Answers will vary. Possible answers: Videotaping my presentations is somewhat similar. When I videotape, I feel the pressure to perform well. It is similar to having my classmates watch me. Then I can watch the video and see how I can improve my presentation.

WRITE WHAT YOU THINK
Activity A., B., p. 80
Answers will vary. Possible answers:
1. VR could help me practice role plays where I speak English. VR could also help me learn specific biology lab procedures.
2. Yes, I would like to use VR to improve my English. It would be more realistic than responding to an audio file.

READING SKILL
Activity A., p. 81
Answers for second supporting details may vary.

VR for anatomy Main idea: *Better way to learn the parts of the body*
Supporting idea: *Can see how everything fits together*
Supporting idea: *Can remove layers of muscle*
VR for examinations Main idea: *Can practice before examining a real patient*
Supporting idea: *Student clicks on parts of the body to check*
Supporting idea: *Student can have virtual patient move parts of the body*
VR for emergency room situations Main idea: *Practice for working under pressure*
Supporting idea: *Students must make decisions quickly*
Supporting idea: *Students can see results of their actions*

READING 2
PREVIEW THE READING
Activity A., pp. 82–83
1. ban
2. energy
3. artificial
4. reason
5. advantage
6. equipment
7. invent
8. unfair

Activity B., p. 83
The Technology Advantage: Better Equipment, Better Performance

Activity C., p. 83
Answers will vary. Possible answers: Running sneakers are always improving so that runners can run longer distances, faster. Skis might be changing so that skiers can ski faster. Tennis racquets are lighter than they used to be.

WORK WITH THE READING
Activity B., p. 85
a. 6
b. 4
c. 1
d. 5
e. 3
f. 2
g. 7

Activity C., p. 86
1. They believe that technology makes sports unfair because some people can afford the new technology while others cannot.

2. Swimmers could swim faster.

3. Swimmers began breaking many records.

4. FINA banned the swimsuits.

5. Fewer records were broken.

6. artificial legs, contact lenses, special shoes

Activity D., p. 86

1. F The graph shows the fastest times for women swimmers between 1998 and 2017.

2. F The slowest time was 1998 and the fastest was 2017.

3. T

4. T

5. F Overall, times have decreased by about 2 seconds between 2012 and 2017.

Activity E., p. 86
Answers will vary.

1. They can swim faster. They can break records. They float better.

2. Swimmers may be benefiting from better training or better swimming techniques. They are stronger.

WORK WITH THE VIDEO
Activity B, p. 87

1. T

2. F (the satellites orbit the earth)

3. T

4. T

5. F (it uses the speed of the signal and the time it takes to travel from the satellite to the receiver)

6. F (three satellites are needed)

7. T

Activity C, p. 87

1. Answers will vary.

2. Answers will vary. Possible answer:
GPS can make emergency vehicles reach their destination faster and therefore potentially save lives.

WRITE WHAT YOU THINK
Synthesize, p. 88
Answers will vary.

1. I think the Olympic Games are not completely fair because some countries cannot afford to train their athletes as well as other countries. Also, sometimes athletes compete for countries that they are not even from because they were not able to get on their country's team.

2. Lots of training and advice from coaches can improve an athlete's performance. I think a family's support can make the biggest difference.

VOCABULARY SKILL
Activity A., p. 89

1. against, with, for, in

2. **a.** against, with **b.** for **c.** with **d.** in

3. "They had to compete against several larger companies to get the contract."

4. Answers will vary.

Activity B. p. 89

1. noun, adjective

2. adjective

3. noun, verb, adjective

4. abilities

WRITING SKILL
Activity A., pp. 90–91

1. "In my opinion, sports organizations ought to have rules against contact lenses in competitions." *In my opinion* signals the opinion.

2. In the first few sentences

3. Contact lenses give some players an unfair advantage; Contact lenses are too expensive for many golfers.

4. *For this reason* and *is another reason*

5. The concluding sentence restates the topic.

Activity B., p. 91
Opinion: Sports organizations ought to have rules against contact lenses in competitions.
Reason: They can give athletes an unfair advantage.
Supporting Details: Eyesight is extremely important. Super-vision allows them to play better than others.
Reason: High-tech contact lenses are very expensive.
Supporting Details: Players who cannot afford these contact lenses are at a disadvantage.

Activity C., p. 92
Answers will vary.

Activity D., p. 93
Answers will vary.

Activity E., p. 93
Answers will vary.

GRAMMAR
Activity A., p. 94
Ought to is used in the topic sentence. *Must* is used in the concluding sentence.

Activity B., p. 94
Answers will vary.

1. should/ought to; VR gives students more practice before they take care of real patients

2. should not; VR technology is very expensive and is not good for all types of courses

3. should; it may help them improve their performance

4. ought to/should; they need to decide if improvements are safe and fair

UNIT ASSIGNMENT
PLAN AND WRITE
Activity A., p. 95
Answers will vary.

Activity B., p. 95
Answers will vary.

Activity C., p. 96
Answers will vary.

The Q Classroom

Activity A., p. 99
Answers will vary. Possible answers:
1. My neighbor owns a family business. It's a dry cleaners. I think it's successful because it is usually busy. I don't know if it makes a lot of money, though.
2. An older man and a young man (possibly father and son) work together at a bakery. Teaching the young man how to make good bread can help the business continue to be successful in the future.

Activity B., p. 99
1. Sophy's uncle's business is successful because it's the only place in the area where you can get Persian food.
2. Answers will vary. Possible answer: Family members may care more about the business and work harder.

READING 1
PREVIEW THE READING

Activity A., pp. 100–101
1. courage
2. design
3. expert
4. unity
5. expand
6. strength
7. corporation
8. manage

Activity B., p. 101
Answers will vary. Possible answers: The article is probably about a manufacturing company. Advantages: you can trust your family; family members will work hard; the family stays together. Disadvantages: family members may argue; the family may lose money.

Activity C., p. 101
Answers will vary. Sample answer: I wouldn't like to work in a family business. My sister and I don't always agree. I think we would fight too much. In order for a family business to succeed, family members have to be able to work together without getting frustrated.

READING SKILL

Activity B., p. 101
Answers will vary. Possible answer: Abdullah Al Hamad Al Zamil started a business. His sons were part of the business. They were modest and worked hard. The family business is now a huge corporation. While it's hard for a family business to be strong for many years, the Zamil family business is very successful.

Activity C., p. 102
1. Reading 2
2. Reading 1
3. Reading 2
4. Reading 1 and Reading 2
5. Reading 2

WORK WITH THE READING

Activity B., p. 103
1. b
2. a
3. c

Activity C., p. 104
a. 3
b. 5
c. 4
d. 1
e. 2

Activity D., p. 104
1. trading
2. food
3. textiles
4. expand
5. successful
6. invested
7. design
8. hardworking
9. risks
10. corporation

Activity E., pp. 104–105
1. He was 19.
2. Their success is thanks to strong family relationships, a feeling of unity, and sharp business sense.
3. He taught them to be modest, honest, hardworking, and respectful, and to take risks from time to time.
4. They wanted to expand their business.
5. No. They are separated to keep the company strong.

Activity F., p. 105
a. 3
b. 5
c. 8
d. 2
e. 1
f. 7
g. 4
h. 6

WRITE WHAT YOU THINK

Activity A., B., p. 105
1. Answers will vary. Possible answer: Family unity, sharp business sense, hard work, expertise in new technologies, and keeping owners and managers separate helps the Zamil family have a successful business.
2. Answers will vary. Sample answer: When I work with a group of people, I am a good listener. I like talking with people, and I am curious about what they think. I help each person participate. I'm also a good writer, so I often take notes for the group.

READING 2
PREVIEW THE READING

Activity A., pp. 106–107
1. b
2. b
3. a
4. a
5. a
6. b
7. a
8. b
9. b
10. a

Activity B., p. 107
Paragraph 4

Activity C., p. 107
Answers will vary. Possible answers: A family business might not be successful because it isn't carefully planned. It might be poorly managed. Family members might not have clear responsibilities.

WORK WITH THE READING
Activity B., p. 109
1. <u>F</u>; Paragraph 1 Seventy percent of family businesses fail, and the owners cannot pass down the businesses to their sons and daughters.
2. <u>T</u>; Paragraph 2
3. <u>T</u>; Paragraph 2
4. <u>F</u>; Paragraph 4 The family let people outside of the family manage the newspaper.

Activity C., p. 109
1. 85; 30; 20
2. First pie chart:
15%: Businesses that are not family-owned
85%: Family-owned businesses
Second pie chart:
70%: Family-owned businesses that fail within 20 years
30%: Family-owned businesses that will last more than 20 years

Activity D., p. 109
Answers may vary. Possible answers:
Family members do not have clear responsibilities.
Families are not realistic about the dreams and goals of the younger generations.

WORK WITH THE VIDEO
Activity A., p. 110
Answers will vary.

Activity B., p. 110
1. 170
2. father, son
3. Zurich
4. factory
5. chocolate-maker
6. machine
7. quality
8. biggest

WRITE WHAT YOU THINK
Synthesize, p. 111
1. Answers will vary. Possible answer: Advantages: Everyone has a stake in the businesses success. You can trust your family. Disadvantages: It can lead to some disagreements in the family. Some family members may take advantage of the situation.
2. Answers will vary. Possible answer: Small businesses can't afford rent. There aren't enough customers, and the businesses don't make enough money.

CRITICAL THINKING SKILL
Activity A., p. 112

Source	
Reading 1	have courage to expand the business; separate the owners from the managers; have strong family values
Reading 2	have good management; have clear responsibilities; be realistic about goals
Unit video	be careful about quality; develop new products
Own ideas	(Answers will vary.)

Activity B., p. 112
Answers will vary. Possible answer: There are several keys to making a family business successful. First of all, family members need to teach younger people the skills of the business. It is also important that each family member has clear responsibilities and that everyone agrees about what needs to be done. A family business needs to have realistic goals, but they also need to take risks sometimes.

Activity C., p. 112
Answers will vary.

VOCABULARY SKILL
Activity A., p. 113
1. advice, darkness, furniture, happiness, information, luggage, news, police, traffic
2. **a.** analyses **b.** cacti/cactuses **c.** children **d.** lives
3. **a.** broke down **b.** burst into **c.** shone at

WRITING SKILL
Activity A., p. 115
1. Many workers today have different options about how and where they work.
2. There are four supporting sentences. <u>Thanks to technology, some people can live far away from their offices and work from home. Computers and the Internet make it possible for individuals to telecommute—that is, to use the telephone and technology to get their work done without being in the office. In addition, since most computers now have microphones and video cameras, it is easy to have a meeting even when people are far away from each other. Now if someone gets a new job, they may not have to move to a new city.</u>
3. Yes, all of the sentences are about the same idea.

Activity B., p. 115
People from the same family are sometimes quite different. Perhaps the father is usually quiet, while the mother is likely to be noisy. Brothers and sisters can also have very different personalities. ~~Two brothers might both be very funny.~~ There can also be large differences in appearance. Some family members may be tall, while others are short. ~~Perhaps they have similar hair or faces.~~ As you can see, family members may not be very similar at all.

Activity C., p. 115
1. First
2. Next / In addition
3. For instance
4. In addition / Next
5. Finally

Activity D., p. 116
1. The writer is going to start a new math tutoring business.
2. There are three transition phrases: *first; in addition; finally*
3. No. This sentence does not support the main idea: *I hope to major in business when I attend college.*
4. Answers will vary. Students may ask questions about the price of each class, what materials the writer will use for teaching, and if the writer will hire any additional employees.

Activity E., p. 116
Answers will vary.

Activity F., p. 117
Answers will vary.

GRAMMAR
Activity A., p. 118
1. simpler
2. safer
3. clearer
4. prettier
5. bigger
6. more realistic

Activity B., p. 118
1. more successful
2. more responsible
3. more intelligent
4. friendlier
5. faster

Activity C., p. 118
Answers will vary. Possible answers:
1. Basketball is the most interesting sport to watch.
2. Pho is the most delicious food in the world.
3. Spring is the most beautiful season in the year.
4. Soccer is the most difficult sport to play.
5. Petra is the most famous place in my country.

UNIT ASSIGNMENT
PLAN AND WRITE
Activity A., p. 119
Answers will vary.

Activity B., p. 119
Answers will vary.

Activity C., p. 119
Answers will vary.

The Q Classroom
Activity A., p. 123
Answers will vary. Possible answers:
1. I would want to be able to remember new words better.
2. Some students learn more easily because they study hard and do their homework.
3. A group of people are studying together. I prefer to study with a group. I remember things better when I discuss them and I can ask questions when I'm not sure about something.

Activity B., p. 123
1. Felix wants to improve his reading. He wants to read faster and know more vocabulary words.
2. Sophy wants to be able to listen better and record new information.
3. Answers will vary.

READING 1
PREVIEW THE READING
Activity A., p. 124
1. benefit
2. automatically
3. skip
4. decrease
5. comfort zone
6. process
7. interact
8. pace
9. provide
10. unique

Activity B., p. 125
The blog post will be about learning to read faster and better.

Activity C., p. 125
Answers will vary.

WORK WITH THE READING
Activity B., p. 127
Sentences 1 and 3 should be circled.

Activity C., p. 127
1. T; Paragraph 1
2. F; Paragraph 2 Moving your mouth slows down your reading.
3. F; Paragraph 3 You should skip over words you don't know and look them up later.
4. F; Paragraph 3 If you translate everything from English to your own language, it will slow you down.
5. T; Paragraph 4
6. T; Paragraph 6
7. T; Paragraph 8

Activity D., pp. 127–128
Answers will vary. Possible answers:
1. Reading requires learners to use their eyes and their brains at the same time.
2. They move their mouths or look up the meaning of every new word.
3. The brain can understand groups of ideas better than just single words.
4. Try reading the same passage more than once and time yourself. Use your finger or a piece of paper to make your eyes move down the page more quickly.
5. Mark up your book by writing, underlining, and highlighting.

Activity E., p. 129
Answers will vary.

WRITE WHAT YOU THINK
Activity A., B., p. 128
Answers will vary.

READING SKILL
Activity A., p. 129
c and d

Activity B., p. 129
1. b
2. c
3. a
4. e
5. d

CRITICAL THINKING STRATEGY
Activity A., p. 130
Answers will vary. Possible answers:
1. a magazine article
2. brain, secrets, successful, students, Japan, Turkey, Canada, Russia
3. Students doing various activities: studying, exercising, taking notes in class, teaching other students

Activity B., p. 130
Answers will vary.

READING 2
PREVIEW THE READING
Activity A., pp. 131–132
1. eventually
2. productive
3. access
4. assist
5. physical
6. internal
7. frustrated
8. period
9. respond
10. concept

Activity B., p. 132
The students come from Japan, Turkey, Canada, and Russia.

Activity C., p. 132
Answers will vary.

WORK WITH THE READING
Activity B., p. 134
3. A good way to remember is to study something and then repeat the process.

Activity C., p. 134
1. T; Paragraph 2
2. F; Paragraph 3 Yuki suggests repeating the memorizing activity.
3. F; Paragraph 4 When people don't get enough sleep, they don't learn as well.
4. T; Paragraph 5
5. T; Paragraph 6
6. F; Paragraph 7 Alex likes to have a variety of study locations and times.
7. T; Paragraph 8

Activity D., p. 134
1. Emre
2. Sarah
3. Yuki
4. Alex
5. Emre
6. Alex

Activity E., p. 135
Answers will vary. Sample answers:
1. I agree with Emre. I think sleep and rest are very important.
2. Yes, I think I can use these ideas to become a better learner.
3. I think teachers should take responsibility for the learning of their students.

WORK WITH THE VIDEO
Activity A., p. 135
All answers are correct: thinking, sleep, heart rate, personality

Activity B., p. 135
Brain stem: unconscious processes, digestion, temperature, sleep
Cerebellum: balance, posture
Cerebrum: thought, personality, the senses, voluntary movement

Activity C., p. 135
The cerebrum.

WRITE WHAT YOU THINK
Synthesize, p. 136
Answers will vary. Possible answers:
1. Be sure to save enough time to study before the test. Get enough sleep and exercise. Try to study in short periods and take breaks.
2. Answers will vary.

VOCABULARY SKILL
Activity A., pp. 137–138
Answers will vary. Sample answers:
1. light
Definition 1: the energy from the sun, a lamp, etc.
Sentence: The light was too low for us to see.
Definition 2: something that produces light, for example, an electric lamp
Sentence: Suddenly, all the lights came on.
Definition 3: having a lot of light
Sentence: In the summer, it's still light at 9 o'clock.
Definition 4: pale in color
Sentence: She wore a light blue sweater.
2. row
Definition 1: to move a boat through water using long wooden poles with wide, flat ends
Sentence: He rowed the boat slowly down the river.
Definition 2: a line of people or things
Sentence: The kids were standing in a row at the front of the classroom.
3. tip
Definition 1: the thin pointed end of something
Sentence: The tips of her fingers were blue from the cold.
Definition 2: a piece of useful advice about something practical
Sentence: He had some useful tips about how to save money.
Definition 3: to give a waiter/waitress, taxi driver, etc. an extra amount of money to thank him/her for good service
Sentence: You should tip the waitress about 15% of the bill.

4. bank
Definition 1: an organization that keeps money safely for its customers
Sentence: Is there a bank near here where I can find an ATM?
Definition 2: a supply of things that you keep to use later
Sentence: The company has a data bank of customer names and phone numbers.
Definition 3: the ground along the side of a river or canal
Sentence: People were fishing along the banks of the river.

Activity B., p. 138
Answers will vary depending on the dictionary.

WRITING SKILL
Activity A., p. 139
Here's how to do your math homework. First, get out your textbook or worksheet and look up your assignment. Then carefully read the directions. Next, start to work on the math problems. When you get stuck on a problem, don't be afraid to ask for help. While you are finishing your homework, be careful not to make mistakes. Finally, check your work and prepare to hand it in to your teacher.

Activity B., pp. 139–140
The order of the steps can vary. Sample answer:

Process: How to write a paragraph
Start

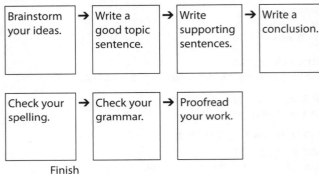

Finish

Activity C., p. 140
To write a paragraph, first brainstorm your ideas. Next, write a good topic sentence and supporting sentences. Write a conclusion. Then check your spelling and grammar. Remember to proofread your paragraph before you hand it in to your teacher.

Activity D., p. 140
Answers will vary.

Activity E., p. 140
Answers will vary.

Activity F., pp. 140–141
Answers will vary.

Activity G., p. 141
Answers will vary.

GRAMMAR
Activity A., p. 142
Creating your own online blog is a good way to connect with people who share your interests. I started a blog last year to share my experience as an international exchange student in Miami, Florida. It was very easy to do, and it allowed me to

practice my writing skills and be in touch with other students. Here's how you do it. First, go online (to find) free blog websites. There are many available, but you should look for one that is easy to use. Start by looking at some sample blogs (to get) ideas for your own blog. Then get started! The site will tell you what to do for each step of the set-up process. After you have set up your blog, you can write your first post. Use photos (to add) visual interest to your page. Having a blog is a fun experience because you get comments from people who read it. It's also a great way to practice your writing skills and to think creatively.

Activity B., pp. 142–143
Answers will vary. Sample answers:
1. I use the internet to find information, to read the news, and to stay in touch with my friends.
2. I use a GPS to find new places in the city. I use it because it's easier to use than maps.
3. Students want to read faster to save time doing their homework.
4. I am studying English to improve my chances of getting a job.

UNIT ASSIGNMENT
PLAN AND WRITE
Activity A., p. 143
Answers will vary.

Activity B., p. 143
Answers will vary.

Activity C., p. 144
Answers will vary.

The Q Classroom
Activity A., p. 147
Answers will vary. Possible answers:
1. Parks, vegetable gardens, flower gardens, street trees, small lakes, river, walkway along the river, and so on. Wild animals include birds, squirrels, raccoons, and insects.
2. I think that cities need some nature. But housing and transportation are more important than parks.

Activity B., p. 147
1. Examples included: trees, bushes, grass, rivers, ponds, animals, and birds.
2. No, they didn't. Sophy and Felix thought it was important to have nature in the city. Yuna said that parks use too much land and that we need more apartments.
3. Answers will vary.

READING 1
PREVIEW THE READING
Activity A., p. 148
a. divided into
b. emotional
c. attitude
d. found that
e. benefit
f. relax
g. experience
h. generous
i. unable
j. a better understanding

Activity B., p. 149
Answers will vary. Possible answers: A woman is walking some dogs. Families are playing in the playground.

Activity C., p. 149
Answers will vary.

WORK WITH THE READING
Activity B., p. 151
1. Paragraph 3 They found out that after walking in nature, people had different brain activity and did better on memory tests.
2. Paragraph 4 More and more people live in cities and they have more mental health problems.
3. Paragraph 5 They became more generous with their money and more interested in community.
4. Paragraph 5 Yes, parks encourage more social connections.
5. Paragraph 6 No, you don't need a large park.

Activity C., p. 151
Answers will vary. Possible answer: The main idea of this article is that nature influences city residents in positive ways.

READING SKILL
Activity A., p. 152
1. e, Paragraph 5
2. b, Paragraph 4
3. a, Paragraph 3
4. c, Paragraph 4
5. d, Paragraph 5

Activity B., p. 153
1. Freeways are important for transportation in large cities, but sometimes, they bring too much traffic, noise, and pollution. This was true of the Cheonggye Freeway in Seoul, South Korea. Built in 1968, the freeway covered Cheonggye Creek. By the 1990s, the Cheonggye Freeway was a major urban problem. In the early 2000s, the city removed the freeway and started a new, fast bus service. Now a beautiful artificial creek flows through the city. It has helped the environment. It also improved the tourist economy. Removing this major freeway has improved the quality of life for Seoul residents.
2. Freeways are important for transportation in large cities, but sometimes, they bring too much traffic, noise, and pollution. This was true of the Cheonggye Freeway in Seoul, South Korea. Built in 1968, the freeway covered Cheonggye Creek. By the 1990s, the Cheonggye Freeway was a major urban problem. (b) In the early 2000s, the city removed the freeway and started a new, fast bus service. Now a beautiful artificial creek flows through the city. It has helped the environment. (a) It also improved the tourist economy. (c) Removing this major freeway has improved the quality of life for Seoul residents.
3. a

Activity C., p. 154
Answers will vary.

WRITE WHAT YOU THINK
Activity A., B., p. 154
Answers will vary.

READING 2
PREVIEW THE READING
Activity A., p. 155
1. wildlife
2. remarkable
3. connected
4. As a result
5. government
6. plant
7. surround
8. ancient

Activity B., p. 156
Answers will vary. Possible answers: Singapore, Cairo, and Vancouver have all added nature for their residents to enjoy.

Activity C., p. 156
Answers will vary.

WORK WITH THE READING
Activity B., p. 158
3

Activity C., p. 158
Answers for *interesting fact* will vary.

City	Notes
2. Cairo	
Population	12 million people
Unique features	surrounded by desert and salt water; ancient city
Nature	added park with plants, trees, pools, lake
Interesting fact	was built on a 500-year old trash dump
3. Vancouver	
Population	2.5 million people
Unique features	seaside city; densely populated
Nature	adding trees; rewilding areas; more bike lanes
Interesting fact	over 800 miles of bike lanes

Activity D., p. 159
1. a **2.** c **3.** b **4.** b **5.** c

Activity E., p. 159
1. The government required all new buildings to have plants and trees. It also helped to build the Gardens by the Bay.
2. It approved the Greenest City Action Plan with goals to protect the environment. It is important for a city to have a plan so that it can make good decisions.
3. It was 20 years. It took a long time to find a location. Also, it probably took time to design the park and get together all of the money. Building the park took time, too.
4. Answers will vary.
5. Answers will vary.

WORK WITH THE VIDEO
Activity A., p. 160
Answers will vary.

Activity B., p. 160

Omaha, Nebraska	Detroit, Michigan	New York, New York
Dan and Andrew are from here people used to grow their own food	first city in the road trip many empty lots people don't have enough fresh food	second city in the road trip not much empty space space for gardens on rooftops

Activity C., p. 160
Answers will vary. Possible answers:
1. I think the idea of using empty spaces would work in my town. There are some parks with space for a garden. There may also be some rooftops for gardens.
2. It is good to have vegetable gardens in cities because then the vegetables are very fresh. You don't need trucks to transport the vegetables. Also, city gardens help children learn about growing vegetables.

WRITE WHAT YOU THINK
Synthesize, p. 161
1. I think it would be good to add vegetable gardens to our city parks. There is space available. Gardens can help people learn about healthy foods. Also, gardening together helps people get to know each other. I think that Riverside Park would be a good place for a vegetable garden. There is a lot of open space there.

VOCABULARY SKILL
Activity A., pp. 161–162
1. b **2.** a **3.** b **4.** b **5.** a

Activity B., p. 162
2. Please throw your trash away.
3. Put your hat on.
4. I usually clean the kitchen up after dinner.
5. I walk a lot, so I wear my shoes out quickly.

GRAMMAR
Activity A., p. 163
1. single action
2. series of actions
3. repeated action
4. repeated action
5. single action
6. series of actions

Activity B., p. 164
1. interrupted action
2. duration
3. interrupted action
4. duration

WRITING SKILL
Activity A., p. 165
1. 2, 7, 11
2. Sentence 3: Today it is a peaceful park, <u>but</u> it was not always a clean or safe place.
Sentence 5: In the 1900s, there wasn't money to repair the park, <u>so</u> no one took care of the trees and buildings.
Sentence 8: In the late 1970s, a new management company started, <u>and</u> slowly the park was repaired.
Sentence 9: Central Park became a beautiful and safe place again, <u>so</u> people could once again enjoy the park.
Sentence 10: Nowadays, the park is enjoyed by residents and tourists, <u>and</u> it offers people a bit of peace in the middle of New York City.
3. 1
4. 11

Activity B., p. 165
1. Istanbul, Turkey, has over 15 million residents, and it is the country's largest city.
2. Istanbul has many ancient historic sites, but tourists enjoy modern attractions as well.
3. Turkey is between Europe and Asia, so it shares features of many cultures.
4. Istanbul is the largest city, but Ankara is the capital.
5. Turkey has 40 national parks and 189 nature parks.

Activity C., p. 166
Answers will vary. Possible answers:
1. Our city park is not very clean, so people don't visit it.
2. People who ride bicycles in a city have to be careful, and they need to follow traffic rules.
3. In my opinion, trees in a city are nice but not that important.
4. Why should the city spend more money on parks?
5. Don't cut flowers from the city garden.

UNIT ASSIGNMENT
PLAN AND WRITE
Activity A., p. 167
Answers will vary.

Activity B., p. 167
Answers will vary.

Activity C., p. 168
Answers will vary.

The Q Classroom
Activity A., p. 171
Answers will vary. Possible answers:
1. The last time I was sick was in February. I had a very bad cold and a fever. I caught the cold from my cousin.
2. I am careful to eat well and get enough sleep. I also take vitamins.
3. The mask could protect him from getting a virus from another person.

Activity B., p. 171
1. Answers about how often students do these things will vary.
   a. eat right
   b. exercise
   c. wash hands
   d. wear a mask when sick
   e. get vaccinations
   f. stay home
2. Answers will vary.

READING 1
PREVIEW THE READING
Activity A., pp. 172–173
a. related to
b. symptom
c. virus
d. cover
e. infect
f. severe
g. extremely
h. develop
i. cure
j. fever

Activity B., p. 173
Answers will vary.

Activity C., p. 173
Answers will vary.

WORK WITH THE READING
Activity B., p. 175
Main ideas: 1, 4, 8
Supporting details: 2, 3, 5, 6, 7

Activity C., p. 175
1. Paragraph: 2 College students have an average of <u>four to six</u> colds per year.
2. Paragraph: 3 College students get more colds because they live, eat, and study <u>on a college campus</u>.
3. Paragraph: 4 Colds are caused by <u>over 200</u> different types of viruses.
4. Paragraph: 4 A cold is <u>different from</u> the flu (influenza). It is not as severe.
5. Paragraph: 6 People get more colds during cold weather because viruses spread easily in <u>dry</u> air.
6. Paragraph: 7 A sneeze or a cough <u>can</u> spread virus germs.
7. Paragraph: 9 The article suggests that students <u>should not share food</u>.
8. Paragraph: 10 The best thing to do when you catch a cold is <u>to rest and avoid spreading it to others</u>.

Activity D., p. 176
Answers will vary. Sample answer:
1. What medicine can I take for a cold?
2. You can take a decongestant and cough medicine.
3. Answers will vary.

WRITE WHAT YOU THINK
Activity A., B., p. 176–177
Answers will vary. Sample answers:
1. If I feel like I am going to get a cold or the flu, I take extra vitamin C. I also drink herbal tea if I feel like I am getting a cold. I make sure that I get enough sleep, too.
2. I would say 4 on a scale of 1 to 10. I worry a little about getting sick because I don't want to miss work and school.
3. I would like to learn more about diabetes. There are several people in my family with diabetes. I want to know how to avoid getting it.

READING SKILL
Activity A., p. 177
Answers will vary. Sample answers:
1. Answers will vary.
2. a. main idea; b. synthesis; c. detail
3. a. They spread when someone with a cold virus coughs or sneezes and someone else comes into contact with the germs from the cough or sneeze. b. Yes, I will change some of my habits. I will be more careful about washing my hands and covering my mouth when I cough or sneeze. c. The flu is more severe than a cold. You have a high temperature.

Activity B., p. 178
Answers will vary. Sample answers:
1. Yes, because humans do not have protection and there may be no medicine. There is a higher risk of death.
2. It could spread when someone is near or touches a sick animal. This could happen to someone who lives or works on a farm. It spreads quickly from person to person through sneezing and coughing, like other types of flu.

READING 2
PREVIEW THE READING
Activity A., p. 179
1. volunteer
2. treat
3. source
4. risk
5. emergency
6. contaminated
7. Prevention
8. outbreak
9. contagious
10. take steps

Activity B., p. 180
All answers are possible: Share knowledge, use technology, wash their hands, cooperate with others

Activity C., p. 180
Answers will vary.

WORK WITH THE READING
Activity B., p. 181
1. Paragraphs 1, 2. The United States, Haiti, Greece, and West Africa
2. Paragraph 2. The disease was extremely contagious.
3. Paragraph 3. Not enough water or not enough clean water
4. Paragraph 4. More than 2 billion
5. Paragraph 6. The mosquito
6. Paragraph 6. Use mosquito netting

Activity C., p. 182
1. Paragraph. 1. F Dr. Andersson-Swayze usually works in the United States.
2. Paragraph 2. F Ebola is a terrible disease that kills people. It is very contagious.
3. Paragraph 3. T
4. Paragraph 4. F Unclean water is often contaminated by chemicals or human waste.
5. Paragraph 5. T
6. Paragraph 6. T
7. Paragraph 7. F The Gates Foundation has given millions of dollars to help improve public health.
8. Paragraph 8. T

Activity D., p. 182
1. poor
2. care
3. outbreak
4. common
5. water
6. water
7. dehydration
8. malaria
9. mosquitoes
10. netting

Activity E., p. 183
d and e

CRITICAL THINKING SKILL
Activity F., p. 183
2. The outbreak of the Ebola virus killed many people in northwest Africa.

Activity G., p. 183
Answers will vary. Possible answers:
1. Many people become sick because they do not have clean water. They can die from dehydration.
2. Helping people get clean water can prevent disease. It is necessary to educate people about the importance of clean water.
3. Many people die each year from malaria. Mosquito netting is a simple solution to help stop the spread of malaria.

WORK WITH THE VIDEO
Activity A., p. 184
Answers will vary.

Activity B., p. 184
Javid's Experiment
Question: Can you catch a cold from being cold?
Experiment: Go to the top of a mountain and take coats off.
Result: No one caught a cold from being cold.
Helen's Experiment
Question: How far from a sneeze can you catch a disease?
Experiment: Measure distance of sneeze on a bus
Results: 5.5 meters, or 5 rows on the bus

WRITE WHAT YOU THINK
Synthesize, p. 185
Answers will vary. Sample answers:
1. I think if I went to help someone who was sick I would go to Africa. There are many problems there and maybe I could help.

2. I think it should be up to organizations to deal with public health. They have many more resources. An individual doctor can only do so much.

VOCABULARY SKILL
Activity A., p. 186
1. in common
2. comment on
3. participate in
4. increase in
5. contribute to
6. in response to
7. succeed in
8. in favor of

Activity B., p. 186
Sentences will vary. Sample answers:
1. My friend and I have many interests in common.
2. Would you please comment on this article?
3. Pollution contributes to global warming.
4. There is an increase in fog during the fall.
5. I am not in favor of the proposed law.
6. I would like to participate in your class.
7. I succeeded in finishing the book in two days.
8. I got a letter in response to my complaint.

WRITING SKILL
Activity A., pp. 187–188
1. An epidemic is when a large number of people have the same disease at the same time.
2. The Zika virus in Brazil in 2015.
3. a plague
4. Paragraph 4 in Reading 1 does not give a definition of a cold, but explains the symptoms. The paragraph on page 187 contains more statistical information than paragraph 4 in Reading 1. Both paragraphs point out a difference (from the flu; from a plague).

Activity B., p. 188
Answers will vary. Possible answers:
1. A common cold is a respiratory illness that is caused by a virus.
2. Influenza (the flu) is a virus that spreads easily and can make people very sick.
3. Ebola is a serious and highly contagious disease that can cause death.
4. Malaria is a disease that is spread by mosquitoes.

Activity C., p. 188
Answers may vary.
1. cold; which is
2. cold; severe
3. epidemic; cluster
4. contagious; cannot
5. diseases; by insects

Activity D., G., pp. 189–190
Answers will vary.

GRAMMAR
Activity A., p. 191
commonly; efficiently; frequently; immediately; precisely; rapidly; seriously; successfully
1. rapidly
2. successfully

3. efficiently
4. precisely
5. frequently
6. seriously
7. immediately
8. commonly

Activity B., p. 191
Answers will vary.

UNIT ASSIGNMENT
PLAN AND WRITE
Activity A., p. 192
Answers will vary.

Activity B., pp. 192–193
Answers will vary.

Activity C., p. 193
Answers will vary.